"A truly novel approach to solving many of life's problems from two experts in the field. This short fable presents a framework that covers significant concepts in a simple manner allowing the reader to apply them immediately. This enjoyable book could bring about profound change."

—Professor Steve Peters
Author of 'The Chimp Paradox'

"Whether you are trying to win Olympic gold or manage the demands of being a busy Mum, we can all find ourselves wrestling with challenging situations. I've been fascinated by psychology for a long time, and I found th[...] [...]ok quick to grasp and easy to a[...] [...]ro-found difference to the way I [...]

[...] Jessica Ennis-Hill
Olympic and World Champion

"Mark and Pete make performance psychology accessible and fascinating. This book explains some of their key insights in a truly memorable way."

—Matthew Syed
Journalist and author of 'Black Box Thinking' and 'Bounce'

"After finishing as England captain in 2012, feeling worn down and exhausted by the demands of the job, I have often wondered whether I might have found a way of dealing better with the day-to-day issues that tended to bombard me and others within the team. Having read this fable, I am now sure that there is a better way. Mark and Pete use their vast experience to take you on a journey of discovery that leads to a clear and concise model for dealing with problems in whatever form they come. I will certainly be adhering to these principles in my role of Director of England Cricket."

—Andrew Strauss OBE
Director, England Cricket

PIG

WRESTLING

PIG
WRESTLING

The Brilliantly Simple Way
to Solve *Any* Problem...
and Create the Change
You Need

**PETE LINDSAY &
MARK BAWDEN**

Vermilion
LONDON

1 3 5 7 9 10 8 6 4 2

Vermilion, an imprint of Ebury Publishing,
20 Vauxhall Bridge Road,
London SW1V 2SA

Vermilion is part of the Penguin Random House group of companies whose
addresses can be found at global.penguinrandomhouse.com

Penguin
Random House
UK

Published in the United Kingdom by Vermilion in 2019

www.penguin.co.uk

A CIP catalogue record for this book is available from the British Library

ISBN 9781785042348

Printed and bound in Great Britain by Clays Ltd, Elcograf S.p.A.

Penguin Random House is committed to a sustainable future for our business,
our readers and our planet. This book is made from Forest Stewardship
Council® certified paper.

For our families.

CONTENTS

PREFACE

So tell us, what is it for you? What's the change that you're trying to create?

What is it that's standing in the way of you achieving your goals, from fulfilling your potential, both personally and professionally?

Perhaps it's a situation that you've wrestled with for some time, or maybe it's something that's simply gotten the better of you more recently. The truth is, we all have something that we struggle with from time to time.

It was ten years ago, when we first asked ourselves this simple question…

"What if you could create the change that you need, whatever that may be, by this time next week—if that was the case, what else would have to be true?"

At that time, we could never have known how that 'thought experiment' would result in us questioning everything we believed about change, and the problems that people wrestle with.

Over the following decade, we explored and researched an incredibly diverse range of disciplines and fields. We spent time with experts from the worlds of philosophy, psychotherapy, systems thinking, behavioural economics, family therapy, design thinking,…even the world of magic.

Using these insights, we analysed our own work with elite athletes, teams and business leaders, exploring how some individuals manage to create meaningful change, whilst others, despite seemingly having more resources at their disposal, find themselves stuck.

As a result of all of these experiences we've come to believe that there is one reason, and one reason alone, why individuals struggle to create the change that they need. It's a reason that is common to all individuals, and to every problem that they wrestle with.

We'd now like to share this with you, along with everything else that we've learnt about creating change.

This book represents the first step on that journey.

Pete Lindsay & Mark Bawden
Hathersage, 2017

INTRODUCTION

When we first meet with a new client, we know very little about them.

We have no idea what challenge they've been wrestling with, or what change they're trying to create. We don't know if their problem will be personal or professional. Whether it will be public or private. Whether it will involve just them or a larger group of people.

What we do know, is that in order to enjoy more success in changing times, it's important that each of us is able to create the change that we need.

But sometimes, a situation simply gets the better of us.

Despite our best efforts and intentions, in spite of considering every avenue available to us, we seemingly find ourselves no further forward. Frustrated, fatigued and at a loss about how to proceed, we might reluctantly conclude there is nothing more than can be done. That *that* is simply how the world is.

In the course of our work, we've come into contact with many highly successful people who, despite their prowess in certain domains, have nevertheless found themselves 'stuck' when trying to bring about change in other parts of their lives.

In working with these people, we've had the opportunity to study the characteristics of the problems that seem to bewitch even the best of us. Along the way, we've identified the various thinking traps that we can all too easily fall into, along with the assumptions that continue to hold many of us captive.

More importantly, we've also been able to discover a number of practical routes to getting 'unstuck', helping even the most frustrated of us in taking meaningful steps forward once again.

Thankfully, it transpires that these hard won lessons can actually prevent us getting stuck in the first place. By remaining mindful of these principles, and consistently applying them in our daily lives, each of us can continue to thrive in increasingly fast-moving and complex times.

Using the simple fable that follows, we'd like to share these lessons with you.

Fables are great devices to convey complex and powerful messages in simple and coherent ways. Over the course of this short story, you'll learn a series of key principles and strategies that will help you create the change that you need.

We've crafted these elements into an easily remembered, if slightly bizarre, framework which is contained within the fable. Based on our experience of teaching and applying it, we're confident that you'll be able to recall all of the elements within this framework after just one reading. From that moment on, you'll have those tools immediately to hand, ready to be deployed whenever and wherever you might need them.

Having learnt this approach, some of our clients have found great benefit in incorporating specific aspects or principles into their working practices. But whilst the lessons contained in this fable are based on our work with top businesses and performers, we have found the approach to be just as applicable to everyday scenarios, helping people live healthier, happier and more productive lives.

However you choose to use them, we sincerely hope you enjoy learning and applying these lessons. In doing so, may they help you and those around you in avoiding the perils of Pig Wrestling.

WRESTLING

The Young Manager stormed into his office, slamming the door shut behind him. An unprofessional display, perhaps, but in his present mood it was all he could do not to tear it from its hinges with his teeth. His heart was pounding in his chest, and even his airy, well-lit workspace felt close and claustrophobic. He had reached the end of his tether. It was fight-or-flight time.

He strode to the window and gazed down at the glass-roofed meeting space in the old turbine hall below. The Collective was a business hub for start-ups and small companies, based in a converted power station in the old industrial quarter. Its red-brick chimneys had long since stopped smoking, but it still generated a sort of energy, fuelled by the dreams of its ambitious occupants and fed back into the economic grid of a city that had grown up around it.

The Young Manager had loved coming here in the months since his company moved in. He loved the entrepreneurial drive that the Collective's tenants shared, the determination

1

and creativity of the people who walked the halls. But today, he'd had enough.

The long nights, the years of diligence, and the many hits of coffee it had taken to get him where he was...*none* of it mattered. This time, he was ready to walk.

Oh, he'd faced his fair share of challenges over the years. But he'd always dealt with problems head on, confident that a solution could be found, and his confidence had always been rewarded. But not this time. This one had beaten him.

It came down to a clash of personalities. Two teams of people as difficult and stubborn as they were passionate and professional. Meetings had morphed from a place where ideas were incubated into a confrontational battle of wills. Morale was so low that you had to crane your neck to see rock bottom.

And where, the Young Manager wondered, must the blame be laid? Where else but at the Captain's feet. He had failed. Should he go down with the sinking ship? Or take to the lifeboats and hope for the best?

All manner of advice had been offered as the problem worsened. Friends and colleagues had suggested coaching and mentoring, workshops, incentives, performance management, and top-down restructuring. The Young Manager had listened carefully and considered his options thoroughly. He had pursued his chosen strategies with his habitual confidence and enthusiasm. But despite his best efforts, nothing he tried had any long-term impact on the war of attrition waged by a tribal and uncooperative staff.

As his optimism waned, the Young Manager came to believe that he was overlooking some fundamental aspect to the problem that he faced. He was deadlocked, and it wasn't just him having this problem. Across the business, from department to department, he found himself increasingly mired in long conversations about organisational problems. Cultural change was proving hard to effect, while a drop in staff engagement played heavily on team leaders throughout the company. These were complex situations, and emotions often ran high as an atmosphere of blame and denial began to take hold.

For all his expertise—for all the qualifications he had earned and the advice he had been given—the Young Manager felt like he was no closer to a solution than he had ever been. People grew accustomed to the way things were done in any organisation and came to accept them, even when company practices were deeply flawed. That's why smooth and successful change was so hard to achieve. Maybe you just can't teach an old dog new tricks, he thought to himself as he stared down from his window.

He sighed deeply as his eyes settled on the shingled roof of the tiny coffee shack based at the far end of the turbine hall. The smallest business at the Collective might also have been the busiest, serving freshly ground coffee to the building's caffeine-fuelled workers from dawn to well beyond dusk, but right now it was quiet.

"Dog tricks can wait," said the Young Manager out loud as he turned towards his office door. "I need a coffee."

GROUNDING

The Young Manager walked briskly through his office, avoiding eye contact, not wanting to stop. He took the glass stairs down to the open atrium and lifted his chin to meet the smiling gaze of the Barista as he strode towards him.

The Barista who owned and operated the Courtyard Coffee Shack was a towering, jovial man of perhaps seventy years old. He was unusually spritely for his size, and his youthful, bright-eyed manner made it difficult to gauge his true age. Apart from the lack of a bushy white beard and his attire—which was closer to gentleman's club than Christmas grotto—he would have made a reasonable Saint Nick.

The Young Manager did not know the Barista. He was accustomed to letting his PA pop down to fetch their morning coffee when she had a cheeky cigarette. So he was surprised to hear his order preempted as he approached the wood-panelled kiosk.

"Good morning, sir," boomed the Barista, his voice echoing around the cavernous turbine hall. "Flat white to go, if I'm not mistaken."

The Young Manager nodded, ran his thumb over his smartphone screen, and bumped it against the reader on the coffee shack's counter.

"Do you know everyone's drink in the building?" he asked, casually, trying to remember the last time he had visited the shack in person.

"Of course, sir," said the Barista, "customer loyalty is the backbone of my business. What would it say about me if I could not remember the one thing they ask me for? Now, if you'll excuse me, I have not yet found a way to satisfy my customers' requests without, albeit briefly, *turning my back* on them."

The Barista grinned from ear to ear, showing a wide expanse of neat white teeth, then nodded to the Young Manager and turned to face the shining chrome boiler of his coffee machine. He ground fresh coffee beans and spooned them into the filter basket, tamping them down lightly as the Young Manager began to fiddle with his phone. Next, he lowered the steam wand into a jug of milk and swilled it gently as it heated. The Young Manager's phone rang, and he let out an irritated sigh. He glanced at the screen and rolled his eyes as he swiped it to send an "unavailable" message to the caller.

"Bad day, sir?" asked the Barista without turning around.

"Ha," snorted the Young Manager, drumming his fingers on the countertop impatiently. "Bad few months, more like. Same old problem, though. Nothing new. I suppose I should be used to it by now."

"In my experience"—said the Barista, as he blended fresh espresso with the steaming hot milk—"getting used to a problem can be a problem itself."

"No doubt," replied the Young Manager, "but I've tried every trick in the book, and nothing works."

"Hmm," said the Barista.

"'Hmm,' what?" said the Young Manager, defensively. "You sound doubtful."

"Pardon me, sir," said the Barista, placing the perfectly finished flat white on the counter. "It's really not my place to comment."

"Maybe not, but I wish you would," said the Young Manager. "I'm out of ideas and open to suggestions, *wherever* they come from."

A smile played over the Barista's lips. He was accustomed to being underestimated.

"It's just that, generally speaking," he began, leaning one stout arm on the coffee-shack counter, "people who think they've tried everything to solve a problem have done nothing of the sort. They may have exhausted their own imaginations, but they have not yet tried the *right* thing. Or, indeed, there would not still be a problem."

"Well, I can assure you there's been no lack of imagination on my part!" the Young Manager snapped. He didn't want to get riled, but who was this gigantic keeper of a glorified drinks trolley to suggest that his efforts had fallen short? How could the Barista possibly know what he had struggled with before reaching this impasse? His phone rang again. No doubt they'd be looking for him in the office. He really should be getting back.

"Forgive me," said the Barista, calmly, and continued, "I'm quite sure that you have exhausted every avenue open to you, sir. But perhaps it's time to start thinking about the ones you've kept closed."

The Young Manager knitted his brow and puffed out his cheeks. The Barista's cryptic pronouncements were not providing him with any answers, but there was something about the big man's manner that had him hooked.

"There are many ways to look at a problem," the Barista continued, arching one fluffy, snow-white eyebrow. "Sometimes you have to look at it from another angle before you can be sure you know the shape of the thing."

"I'm not sure where this is going," admitted the Young Manager, "but all right. You've got me. Go on."

"You first," said the Barista. "Tell me a little more about your situation. If nothing else, it seems to me that you could use the opportunity to get things off your chest."

The Young Manager stared at his steaming coffee and nodded. The Barista was right. He was so stressed out that he hadn't slept properly for weeks. He felt like a tightly coiled spring in a rice-paper bag. Everything was threatening to burst out at once.

"Actually," he said, looking up from his drink and smiling weakly, "I'd appreciate that." He took a deep breath and ordered his thoughts. "It comes down to this…I've got two teams—both high performers but from different parts of the business—and they need to work together on a major project. But will they? Can they? Ha! They fight like a high-school yearbook committee. The tension in their teams is off the scale. And that project? Going badly. You know, one of our receptionists actually cried this morning, and this is no shrinking violet. The girl's tough. But this situation…I swear I'll end up in a tribunal."

He massaged his temples where the first nagging tingle of a headache was forming.

"We changed location for a fresh start," he continued. "Figured the old space was *not conducive* to teamwork. But we've still got the same old problems, and it's starting to hit our bottom line. It's holding us back."

The Young Manager took a sip of his coffee and cracked a smile, then waved his hand dismissively.

"But that's just one problem of many, to be honest. I'm wrestling with a host of other issues across the business, and I can't seem to resolve any of them. Maybe I've lost it, you know? Maybe I'm just not cut out for this game."

"Oh, I doubt that," said the Barista, encouragingly. "What about these other issues, then? Care to share?"

"Are you sure?" asked the Young Manager. "It's probably a bit complicated and dull."

The Barista chuckled warmly. "I'll be the judge of that," he said.

"Okay then, but you asked for it," the Young Manager teased. "So, for instance, the leadership team that I'm part of has been trying to implement a cultural-change programme across the organisation as a whole. In essence, we want to move away from the notion of departmental separation and get our staff to share their expertise and collaborate more freely. We overhauled our whole IT set up to make it happen, which *wasn't* cheap. And we ran a series of workshops and roadshows to train the staff in new tools and procedures. And nothing's changed at all! All I hear is managers sick of nagging their staff to get on board and staff resentful of every request."

The old barista nodded sympathetically.

"Then there's the engagement scores," the Young Manager continued, gritting his teeth. "After last year's all-staff survey results, we tried everything to improve employee engagement. But apparently, no amount of resources poured into the problem can make a dent in it."

"Not an uncommon problem," said the Barista.

"I know that's a lot. And maybe we *have* made some headway, but not enough, that's for sure," the Manager went on, lost in his own train of thought. He sipped his coffee and stared into the cup, dejected. "We really do have some good people here, you know? It's just these problems seem to take up so much of everyone's time and energy. I never thought I'd hear myself say this, but for the first time ever, I'm about ready to walk."

"Ah, that's a feeling I recognise," the Barista replied in a fatherly tone. "You'll bounce back. Personally, I've found that *rock bottom* is the perfect foundation on which to build. Besides," he added conspiratorially, "There's one thing I *know* you haven't tried."

The Young Manager looked up to meet the Barista's smiling eyes.

"There is?" he asked hopefully.

The Barista nodded. "Problem Cleaning," he announced.

"Problem Cleaning?" the Young Manager asked, perplexed. "Have you got a magic mop?"

The Barista ignored the comment and continued calmly.

"Problem Cleaning is an approach developed between myself and several of the firms who call the Collective home. It's been used to tackle many problems like yours."

"With the greatest respect," the Young Manager interjected, "you run a coffee stand. I mean, it's a very *nice* coffee stand. And the coffee's great, but…"

"A *very* nice coffee stand, yes," the Barista interrupted, "quite the best in the neighbourhood. I hope you agree. And it brings me into contact with all manner of people and businesses. And, as you may have gathered, I am one of life's listeners. One might imagine that a man of my leanings could learn a great deal over the years. Don't you think?"

"I'm sorry," said the Young Manager. "I didn't mean—"

"I'm sure you didn't," said the Barista. "Now, where was I? Ah yes. Problem Cleaning. I am quite confident that you have not tried our approach yet. In the first place, you say you have tried everything, and yet you haven't been able to create the change that you need. Ergo, you have not yet tried everything. And in the second place, you seem quite certain that you know precisely what your problems are. That certainty, if I may be so bold, is unjustified."

"Now you're really losing me," said the Young Manager, scratching his head.

"Do you like jokes?" asked the Barista, and not waiting for a reply, he continued, "I do. Maybe you've heard this one.

A man stumbles out of his favourite bar at two a.m., staggers a few paces from the door, and SMACK! He walks face first into a lamppost. He picks himself up, dusts himself off, takes two steps forward, and SMACK! Straight back into the same lamppost. The man sits on the ground for a moment or two, catching his breath. Then he shakes away the cobwebs, clambers to his feet, sets off again, and SMACK! Now he's lying on the ground with a bloody nose and torn trousers. He looks up at the lamppost and says, 'All right! I give up! You've got me surrounded!'"

The Young Manager laughed. "And I'm the drunk, right?"

"In a sense, yes." The Barista smiled. "You and your colleagues are like anyone who's struggling with a problematic situation. We approach it in the manner we always have, and when our efforts fail, it is tempting to see the problem as insurmountable, rather than to admit to some flaw in our own actions."

"It certainly feels insurmountable," said the Young Manager as his phone sounded in his pocket. He pulled it out without so much as glancing at the screen and pressed the switch on the side that turned the power off. "So what do I do next?"

"The first thing to tackle is what you *don't* do. You *don't* give up," said the Barista. "The truth is that we all find ourselves stuck now and again. In business, in relationships…how you handle it. *That's* what matters. Let me tell you about a little trouble I had a while back. I think it will illustrate the point."

"Go on," said the Young Manager, leaning into the coffee-shack counter.

"Several years ago," the Barista began, "rather more than I care to admit, my wife and I were engaged in a dispute with an extremely difficult neighbour. It began over a seemingly trivial matter, or should have been, but it had escalated to the point where it was all we thought about—a constant source of angst. We reached the point where we were browsing estate agents' brochures, and considering a move, despite the disruption that would have caused to our young family."

"What was the neighbour doing?" asked the Young Manager, intrigued. "Midweek parties? DIY at dawn?"

"Oh no," the Barista replied, "nothing quite so deliberately antisocial. It all came down to the gate we shared. Our house and his were two halves of an older property, with a large shared driveway out the front, left over from the time when it was a single home. Now, we had young children, as well as family pets to worry about, and the gates opened onto a busy road, so we had become accustomed to keeping them shut at all times. It was a habit our previous neighbours, who had small children of their own, had also acquired, and we hoped to encourage our new neighbour to do the same."

"But he wouldn't play ball, I assume," said the Young Manager.

"No, although he wasn't hostile—at least, not at first," said the Barista. "We quickly realised that he wasn't the sociable type, but there were plenty of opportunities to have a neighbourly word with him. So, after the first time I caught my daughter toddling towards the open gateway, I resolved to raise the issue at once. To add to the sense of urgency, a new building site had just been established around the corner, and our road was busy all day with builders' trucks as well as the usual commuters and delivery vans. Anyway, that evening, I knocked on his door and stated my case quite reasonably. I explained my concerns and assumed that my neighbour would comply with my perfectly rational and polite request."

"But he didn't," said the Young Manager.

"No. He ignored my concerns and left it open again the very next day. I was incensed! Less than twenty-four hours after his assurance that he would remember to shut the gates, our neighbour had already broken his promise!"

"So you talked to him again?"

"Not at first," said the Barista. "I gave him the benefit of the doubt, hoping he'd remember his promise. But every morning, as I left for work, I'd find the gates swinging on their hinges. And with each day passing, the sense of frustration and resentment in me built. My wife helped me to see sense. She suggested that he and I had probably got off on the wrong foot, what with me marching over there to nag him about the gate the moment he moved in, and she suggested we try a gentler approach. Our neighbour didn't work weekends, and when his car was at home, the gates remained closed. So in an effort to build bridges, we invited him over to dinner one Saturday night. It was a very pleasant meal, and the conversation was most amiable. So, at the end of the night, I thought I was in a pretty good position to raise my concerns about the gates again. Again, I reminded him of our concerns for the safety of the children and animals, and again, he again promised that he would endeavour to close the gates. In fact, he was almost sniffy about it. Said he *had* done his best to remember, which I must admit rubbed my back up the wrong way, after days and days of finding the damn things hanging open. Nevertheless, we had made a connection now. He had actually *met* the children. So I hoped he might now feel duty bound to pay closer attention."

"I'm guessing he didn't," said the Young Manager.

"Monday rolled around," the Barista continued, "and I spent the day at the office, as usual, and arrived home around six. As I turned into our driveway, I had to slam the breaks on to avoid hitting my three-year-old." He sighed and shook his head. "He'd been playing hide-and-seek with my wife and somehow managed to escape from the back garden through a side gate, like a little Houdini! It was lucky I got home when I did."

"You must have been furious," said the Young Manager.

"That's an understatement. Obviously it wasn't his fault that our child escaped, but that second gate has always provided a safety back up for us, and I was furious that my neighbour just couldn't seem to respect that. So, I parked the car and stormed over to the neighbour's place, hammered on the door, then gave him a piece of mind in no uncertain terms. I was quite incandescent with rage. It was all I could do not to clobber him on the spot."

"I'm not surprised. So did that do the trick?" asked the Young Manager.

"He said the same thing as before. He'd *try*. But I wasn't taking any chances," said the Barista. "I had a sign made that read PLEASE KEEP SHUT, and hung it on one of the gates so he *couldn't* forget. For a few days, it seemed to be working. Then, one morning, I walked outside to find not only had the sign been removed, but the gates were once more wide open."

"He took down the sign? That's outrageous? What did you do next?" said the Young Manager, leaning in on his elbows.

"I'm not going to tell you," said the Barista calmly.

"What?" said the Young Manager. "You can't do that. I want to know what happened! You're supposed to be helping me solve problems, remember?"

"So now you have one more to solve. When you understand Problem Cleaning, you'll soon find the solution to my old neighbourly dispute. You'll be better placed to create the change that you need, too."

"I will?" asked the Young Manager.

"Most assuredly." The Barista smiled. "Suffice it to say that my dispute *was* resolved. Indeed, we lived quite happily as neighbours after that."

"Give me a clue. One hint," said the Young Manager, scratching his chin.

"Just one," said the Barista. "The route to solving this whole thing began when I realised that this problem wasn't about my neighbour."

"It wasn't? Then…"

"Work it out," said the Barista, with a wink.

The Young Manager rocked back on his heels and furrowed his brow.

"I'm not sure where to begin," he said.

BEGINNING

On a small shelf behind the counter of the Courtyard Coffee Shack sat a small statue. A proud looking, well-fed pig, cast in bronze. The Barista lifted it from its spot and placed it carefully on the counter, turning it towards the Young Manager so that he could read the inscription on a small plaque fixed to its plinth.

> *I learned long ago, never to wrestle with a pig.*
> *You get dirty, and besides, the pig likes it.*

The Young Manager read the quote aloud and nodded.

"I've read that somewhere before," he said. "Pig wrestling. Yeah, that's pretty much how I feel right now."

"George Bernard Shaw," said the Barista. "I thought you might find it relevant."

"So what are you saying?" asked the Young Manager. "That I should stop engaging with them altogether? How does *that* work?"

"No, no." The Barista laughed and continued, "That's not it at all. You remember I mentioned *Problem Cleaning*?"

The Young Manager nodded.

"Well, this portly porker here helped to inspire the whole process," said the Barista, patting the bronze pig on the head, fondly. "That quote got me and some of the others at the Collective thinking, and it all grew from there. From little acorns…"

"Or bronze pigs, apparently," said the Young Manager.

The Barista's eyes glinted with mischief. There was something about the enigmatic old man that the Young Manager couldn't quite figure out. He was charming and eloquent, but there was more to it. He had a sort of easy authority and assuredness that seemed out of place behind the counter of a modest kiosk. A confidence and poise that he associated more with blue chip boardrooms. Then again, the Young Manager mused, the Barista ran a coffee stall. His business was thriving. His customers were loyal. His coffee was, it must be said, great! He had set himself a goal—however modest—and accomplished it with apparent ease. Was that not cause for a certain swagger in his manner?

"About those pigs," said the Barista, snapping the Young Manager back to the present. "This is what you must always remember. It's the problematic situations that we wrestle with that are like pigs. People themselves are very rarely the real problem."

The Young Manager narrowed his gaze. "Go on," he said.

"The problems we wrestle with come in all shapes and sizes, but they do share certain characteristics. And you will know for certain when you are pig wrestling because it will feel like you've tried everything. In these situations, it feels as though nothing has worked and you are at a complete loss about what to do next. As a result, these kind of problems are emotionally draining and tend to feel like they have been around forever. You get the picture?" said the Barista.

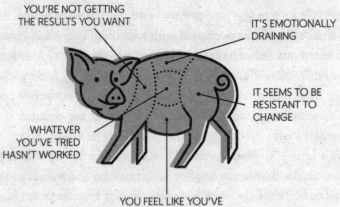

YOU'RE NOT GETTING
THE RESULTS YOU WANT

IT'S EMOTIONALLY
DRAINING

IT SEEMS TO BE
RESISTANT TO
CHANGE

WHATEVER
YOU'VE TRIED
HASN'T WORKED

YOU FEEL LIKE YOU'VE
TRIED EVERYTHING

"Now, it might seem strange, but one of the main reasons that managers find it hard to tackle certain problems is often down to a case of mistaken identity."

"What do you mean by that?" asked the Young Manager.

"Take your situation for example," said the Barista. "Based on what you've told me, you seem to think that you need to learn how to deal with 'dysfunctional teams,' or discover how to foster 'greater engagement,' or improve the 'culture,' or something along those lines."

"But that is what I need," the Young Manager insisted. "Isn't it?"

The Barista smiled. "Is it? What if I told you that you might actually be suffering from a case of *premature evaluation*?"

The Young Manager burst out laughing and blushed at the same time. "I'd ask you to tell me more."

"Well, I've come to believe that there's a single reason why individuals struggle to create the change that they need," the Barista said. "A reason that is common to all individuals, and to every problem that they tackle, and that is…"

Whenever someone finds themselves pig wrestling, the only thing we know for sure is that they're tackling the wrong problem.

The Young Manager allowed the statement to sink in for a moment. "So if that's the case, how would I go about finding the right problem?"

"Now that's a much better question," the Barista replied, tapping the side of his nose and winking. "To do that you need to learn a simple framework. I can teach it to you if that would be useful? It won't take long."

The ground level buzzed to life as people started leaving their offices for their mid-afternoon coffee breaks.

"Really?" the Young Manager asked. He moved aside to let a woman place an order.

"Why don't you come back in the morning and we'll talk then," said the old barista, turning his attention to his customer.

VIEWING

The following morning, the Young Manager arrived at the Collective earlier than usual, and went straight to the Courtyard Coffee Shack. He told himself that he needed the early start to catch up after the previous day, and that a good strong coffee would kick-start him into action, but in fact, he was itching to talk to the Barista again. He'd had a decent night's sleep—his best for a while—but he had woken up with a head still full of strange dreams.

The Barista welcomed him warmly, and listened patiently as the Young Manager poured forth about the visions he had seen.

"For starters," he said, "my staff all had pigs' heads where theirs should have been! Big, wet bristly snouts…piggy little eyes!" He shuddered as he sipped his coffee. "They were taking it in turns to wrestle on the boardroom floor. Becky from Sales was brutal! The rest were cheering her. Baying for blood, practically!" He shook his head as if trying to dislodge the image from his mind.

"It seems to me you have a wonderfully vivid imagination, sir," said the Barista, wiping the counter with a clean white cloth, "a fine attribute in business."

"It's all that stuff you said yesterday," said the Young Manager. "You really got me thinking. Is now a good time to pick the conversation up?"

"Now is *always* the right time, when there's a problem to be solved." The Barista smiled.

The Young Manager pulled a small tablet device and an electronic stylus from his pocket, so that he could take notes this time. The Barista nodded his approval and began.

THE PIG-PEN

"To begin with," he said in his warm, sonorous voice, "I'd like you to picture yourself standing in a lush, green field, at the bottom of a hill. At the top of the hill you can see a pig pen with a wooden fence running round it."

The Young Manager frowned. "Hang on," he said. "This isn't some sort of hypnosis thing, is it? I'm looking for practical solutions. A *framework*, you said, not past life regression."

The Barista chuckled, warmly. "It's nothing like that, I can assure you," he replied. "Now, if you'll only listen, all will become clear. Engage that marvellous imagination of yours. Close your eyes if it helps."

The Young Manager scanned the hall, self-consciously. He wasn't sure he'd want his staff to come across him immersed in a metaphorical meadow. "I'm all right, thanks." he said.

The Barista nodded, cleared his throat and continued:

"As I was saying, imagine yourself in a verdant field at the foot of a hill. And on top of the hill, a fenced pig pen, about the size of a wrestling ring. You climb the hill and approach the pen. You place one foot on the bottom rung of the fence and peer over into the enclosure."

The Young Manager jotted notes as the Barista continued.

"Inside the pen is a huge pig. A real county-fair prize winner, at least three hundred pounds of prime pork, wallowing in the mud.

Then you notice that there's something strange about this particular pig. Its head is sticking through an old wooden picture frame. The frame is wedged tight around the pig's neck. The pig himself seems not to mind, but you can't help feeling that it looks uncomfortable.

With your curiosity piqued, you glance around the pen and, to your left, you find a red plastic bucket, filled with soapy water, and a large sponge. Your gaze moves to the far left corner of the pen, where there is a large, tin feeding trough, filled to the brim with slops. On its side are emblazoned the words *Made in Hanoi*. How are you doing?"

"Pen. Pig. Picture frame. Bucket and sponge. Tin trough. Got it," said the Young Manager.

"Good," the Barista continued, "Now, on the fence post to your right—goodness knows how you missed it before—you notice a gleaming crystal ball, fizzing with magical energy."

The Young Manager furrowed his brow, but the Barista ignored him and went on:

"And opposite it, in the far right corner of the pen, where the soil is firmer and less churned up, you spot a number of gleaming gold nuggets, poking up out of the ground. The pig, you now realise, is eager to reach the gold, but whatever he does, he cannot get any closer. Not just because of the mud, you see, but because of two bright pink bungee cords holding him in place."

"This is getting properly weird," the Young Manager mumbled, as he scribbled on his tablet.

"Stepping back from the fence to take in the whole, bizarre scene, you almost trip over a child's *Spot the Difference* book that has been left on the ground behind you.

Satisfied that you have the measure of the scene before you, you walk to your right, around the pen, passing a large, green recycling bin.

Finally, as you turn to walk away, you notice a bright-yellow warning sign that strikes you as particularly important."

There was a long pause.

"And?" asked the Young Manager.

"And that's it," said the Barista.

"That's what?"

"The framework you asked for," said the Barista, as if it was the most obvious thing in the world, "Every step you need to take to resolve your current problems, or indeed, any problems you might encounter."

"Riiiight" drawled the Young Manager, doubtfully, glancing at the list of nonsensical words he had written down.

"Allow me to explain," said the Barista as he laughed. "The pig pen is merely a memory device used to remember the core elements of our method." He nodded towards the bronze pig statue, back in pride of place, on its shelf behind the counter.

"We needed an image that was striking and a bit, well, a bit silly really. Wilbur here fitted the bill."

"I see," the Young Manager replied, though he wasn't sure he did.

"It's called the Method of Loci," the Barista explained. "Have you heard of it before?"

The Young Manager shook his head.

"A system of memory that dates back to the ancient Greeks and Romans. Perhaps the term *memory palace* is more familiar to you, although it hardly suits our pig pen, does it?"

"Memory palace. That *is* familiar. So how does it work?" asked the Young Manager.

"It's a marvellous trick," the Barista explained, "You place each item that you want to remember at a point along an imaginary journey. The facts to be memorised are converted into bizarre, exaggerated, visual images that are placed along the imaginary journey, fooling your mind into behaving as though it has actually *made* that journey, and storing the information accordingly in a way that it would not for dry facts alone. To recall the information, one walks back through the journey, replacing the visual images that you have memorised with the original facts or items that you associated with them. The more vivid the images you conjure, the more effective they are for retrieving the original data."

"This is all a bit Sherlock Holmes, isn't it?" said the Young Manager.

"Precisely," said the Barista, "Holmes had his own memory palace. Most of us all fall short of the great detective's mental faculties however. Nevertheless, a modest bungalow will suffice. Indeed, even a pig pen."

Rooting around in the pocket of his jacket, the Barista pulled out a piece of paper.

"Ah, here it is," he boomed, "I knew I had it somewhere."

He spread the sheet of paper out flat on the counter and smoothed down the crumpled edges.

"This is a diagram of the pig pen. You can have it, if you like. Run a copy and slip it into your wallet. It will act as an aide memoir, until the layout of the pen becomes second nature."

"You can hang onto the original," said the Young Manager, scrolling to the camera function on his device and taking a snap of the diagram, which he copied across to his notes. "So how do I use this pig pen to solve *my* problems?"

"Every element represents a part of a process," said the Barista, "A set of tools to clean up your thinking and generate new insights. For instance, do you remember the first thing you did after you'd climbed the hill?"

The Young Manager nodded, "I put one foot on the fence, didn't I?"

"Spot on!" beamed the Barista, "Step one of problem solving is what we call *Foot on the Fence Checks*. They're key to ensuring that you're tackling the right problem. Let me explain…"

FOOT ON THE FENCE

"This first step in the process is perhaps the most critical of all," said the Barista, tapping one large finger on the paper in front of him, "Without assessing things fully with your foot on the fence, you might as well dive into the pen and start rolling in the mud with that pig. You won't get anywhere."

"That's certainly how I've felt," replied the Young Manager. "All effort for no reward."

"Well, it's time to stop pig wrestling and climb back out of the pen so you can get a sense of perspective. Give yourself a little distance, and take a good look at this whole picture."

"Standing back from the situation, with one foot on the fence, this is a valuable moment," the Barista said, "Press *pause* and ask yourself some fundamental questions." He paused for a moment himself before continuing. "The first question to ask yourself is…"

How specifically is this a problem for me?

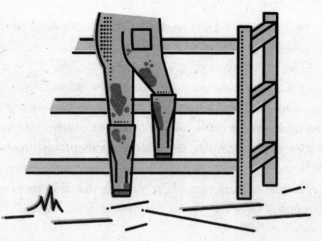

"This helps to focus in on your personal experience of the problem, and the specific issue that you need to address."

The Young Manager nodded and scribbled some notes.

"So much time and energy is wasted in business wrestling with problems that concern us but don't actually *belong* to us," said the Barista, "So step one is ensuring that we focus on our experience of the problem and that the right person or team is on the case."

"That certainly makes sense," the Young Manager agreed, "I've lost count of the number of times I've allowed myself to be drawn into problems that don't affect me directly."

"And that can be very dangerous," explained the Barista. "Because it leads to a culture of gossip and recrimination, and the labelling of colleagues. None of which are remotely helpful."

"But shouldn't I always lend a hand to colleagues who are struggling with their own problems?" asked the Young Manager.

"Of course you should," insisted the Barista. "But you must know where the line is drawn between helping out and shouldering the burden yourself. You'll be much more useful to your staff by helping them clean up their own thinking. You're there to guide, not take over. Anyway, let's assume you have identified the aspect of the problem that *is* yours to own. That brings us to the second Foot on the Fence Check."

"Which is?"

The Barista pointed to the pig in in the middle of his diagram. "One must always ask oneself…"

Have I seen the whites of the pig's eyes?

The Young Manager stopped note-writing and looked up questioningly.

The Barista smiled. "In a team or organisation of any size, a manager will receive an awful lot of their information from second-hand sources. That's inevitable; you can't be everywhere at once. But when it comes to tackling problematic situations, people or processes, second-hand isn't good enough. It's tempting for a well-informed manager with good lines of communication to assume they have the full picture from the moment they hear about a problem, and rush in to try to fix things immediately."

"But isn't that exactly what a leader should do?" asked the Young Manager, "Fix things quickly, I mean."

"As quickly as possible. But that's not going to happen without staring the problem straight in the eye. First-hand information. Don't rely on anyone else's account of the situation; get in there, and take a look at things for yourself."

"Ah, now I see what you mean," said the Young Manager.

"Good," said the Barista, "Let's focus in for a moment. Take people problems. The fact is, you can never hope to understand someone's behaviour, let alone change it, without knowing the specific context in which the behaviour occurred."

"I get that," nodded the Young Manager, "But that's not always possible, is it?"

"Not always," agreed the Barista. "But it is your duty to gain access to as much concrete, first-hand information as possible, not just second, or third-hand storytelling. Storytelling is one of humanity's most wonderful gifts, but we do have a tendency to run away with ourselves, and there's often a tall tale at the heart of a pig-wrestling problem. Misguided attempts to create change often start with a second hand misinterpretation of events."

"So by performing this check, you're making sure you understand the problem first hand." said the Young Manager.

"Precisely," nodded the Barista. "Much less room for misinterpretation that way, and far more scope for influence. Once you've done that, you can move on to the last Foot on the Fence Check…"

Should I tackle this thing right now?

"None of us have unlimited time or energy," the Barista explained. "So what matters is how wisely we put to use the time and energy that we *do* have."

"I get it," said the Young Manager, "Make a judgement call about what *really* needs doing. Prioritising problems is as important as identifying them in the first place."

"You're quite right," the Barista replied, "If the problem has been knocking around for some time already, it might be that you can afford to ignore it, either in the short term or even permanently. It's always worth asking yourself what would happen if you consciously chose to do nothing. Let sleeping pigs lie, so to speak, while you deal with the frontline issues."

"This is taking shape," said the Young Manager swiping the screen of his device to scroll back through his notes, "Let me run through the bullet points so I've got it straight so far."

"Be my guest," said the Barista, with a broad grin.

SUMMARY

- Problems (not people) are pigs. There's a right way and a wrong way to deal with them.

The Young Manager glanced at the Barista who nodded encouragingly.

- Don't get into pig wrestling. If you find yourself wrestling a pig, you know you're tackling the *wrong* problem.
- When you're looking at a pig, run these three checks:

  Check 1: How specifically is it a problem for me?
  Check 2: Have I actually seen the whites of its eyes and got the whole picture?
  Check 3: Should I prioritise this pig right now, and what would truly happen if I did nothing?

"Excellent," boomed the Barista, clapping his hands, "Now, if one were of a cynical disposition, one might consider the ground we've covered so far to be little more than common sense. But in my experience, common sense isn't as common as it should be. Formalising these steps trains one to think in a certain way and facilitates latent talent. Merely keeping these simple principles in mind can avoid wasted weeks, months even entire careers."

"So," said the Young Manager, eagerly, "What's the next step?"

"The next step," the Barista said with a smile, "is for you to meet a few of the people who first climbed into the pig pen with me, so to speak. My original pig wrestlers in this building."

The Young Manager looked at him with surprise. "Really?" he asked, "I had hoped *you* would explain everything." He glanced at his watch. It was nearly nine. A trickle of workers had already started to arrive, and the place would be filling up soon.

"I could," said the Barista with a twinkle in his eye, "However, firstly I believe the lessons ahead will sink in faster if they come from the source. Secondly, it will be good for you to make the acquaintance of other young managers here. And thirdly, in case you hadn't noticed, I have a coffee shack to run."

The Young Manager bounced nervously on his heels, hoping the Barista would have a change of heart, instead, he was handed a thick cream business card with embossed lettering that read:

Gary Cleverly
Picture Framing Service
Unit 4—The Collective

"A couple of hours of your time at most," said the Barista, patting the Young Manager's shoulder, "To learn the habits that will *save* you time and energy every subsequent day of your working life! If you can't recognise that as a good deal then, my friend, business really *isn't* your thing," he chuckled. "Now, Mr. Cleverly is waiting for you. When you're done there, he'll point you in the right direction."

The Young Manager sighed inwardly and forced a smile. He liked the Barista, and the old guy had clearly gone to a lot of trouble to sort these meetings out. But was he really about to spend his morning touring the building when he should have been buckling down at his desk? What was it the Barista had said about priorities? He turned the business card over in his hand, and read the name again: Gary Cleverly.

"Picture Framing, eh?" he said aloud, but the Barista was not listening. The morning rush hour had begun, and he had customers to serve.

Feeling as if he had just been formally dismissed, the Young Manager mumbled a thank you, came to a decision, and set off towards the address on the card.

CLEANING

The Young Manager found Gary Cleverly's picture-framing workshop in a quiet corner of the old power station. The door was ajar and the sound of whistling drifted into the corridor beyond. He listened to it for a moment, trying without success to place the tune, before rapping on the doorframe to announce himself. There was a cheerful "Come in!" from the workshop, and he slid inside to find out who it had come from.

At a work bench on the far side of the room, half buried in picture frames of every imaginable variety, a tall, gangly limbed man with a curly mop of chestnut hair sat scribbling measurements on a scrap of paper. He glanced up at the Young Manager who was hovering near the open door.

"Come on in," he said again, warmly, beckoning the Young Manager forward. "I'll finish this and be right with you."

While Mr. Cleverly worked through his sums, the Young Manager took in the workshop. It wasn't a huge space, but the ceiling was high, and Gary had used wall-to-wall shelves as well as every available surface to cram the room with more stuff than the Young Manager could fathom. The far wall was dominated by a huge circular window through which the morning light poured in. Multi-coloured frame mouldings filled the shelves, packed tightly together arranged by colour like a many-banded rainbow. There were power tools and stacks of reclaimed wood, sheets of glass and mounting card of every size. In the centre of the room were four sturdy work-benches, covered in clamps and cutting equipment, staplers, brushes, and lacquer. Work in progress, the Young Manager concluded. The room was full to bursting point, but for all that, it felt well-organised and well-used. *A place for everything, and everything in its place.*

With his arithmetic completed, Gary tucked his pencil behind one ear and strode over to the Young Manager in two steps of his crane-like legs. He held out his hand to shake, and he smiled.

"Sorry about that," said Gary, shaking the Young Manager's hand vigorously, "Good to meet you. I understand we have a mutual friend."

The Young Manager nodded. "And he told me to come and see you. Are you sure I'm not intruding?"

"Not for a moment," said Gary, "I'm more than happy to help. The more people who get in on this system of ours, the better! So, where are you? You've covered the Pig Pen and the Fence, I take it?"

The Young Manager nodded again.

"Great. Let's get down to the nitty gritty, then. *Problem Cleaning.*"

"Ready," said the Young Manager, taking out his tablet and stylus to continue his notes.

"Do you remember what came after the Foot on the Fence in the scene our friend painted so vividly?"

"I could hardly forget in a room like this," said the Young Manager, gesturing to the shelves and workbenches, "It was a pig, with an old picture frame around its neck, of course."

"Quite right," said Gary. "Come over to my workbench and I'll tell you why that old frame lies at the very heart of all that wrestling you've been doing."

PICTURE FRAME

They crossed the floor to the workstation that Gary indicated. "The truth is," he said, spreading his long fingers and leaning on them over the table top, "Very few of us ever notice the old frames that are hung around the necks of the problems we have to tackle."

"Old frames?" asked the Young Manager.

"Every pig you wrestle with—every supposedly insurmountable problem—is essentially stuck in an old frame. We frame our experiences, the situations we believe we're facing, shaping how we think about them. We tell ourselves that the situation we're tackling is a 'leadership problem,' or a 'cultural problem,' or a 'professionalism problem.' That frame makes it a little easier to make sense of our world. The frame sets the limits and the tone of the contents within it, what's relevant and what isn't, as it does with any picture." He gestured to the framed paintings and sketches scattered around the room.

"I think I see what you mean," the Young Manager nodded, "The frame defines how we are viewing the situation... what kind of problem we think the *problem is.*"

"Exactly. How we view it and how we describe it," said Gary, "All of us create frames to organise and interpret the world around us, and to represent that world to others. They're cognitive shortcuts that help us to make sense of complex situations. Without them, we'd be trying to hold vast amounts of unconnected information in our heads. We'd be overwhelmed. So instead we frame our experiences. That said," Gary continued, "A frame is also a filter. It colours our perception of its contents. And that can be dangerous, because we have a tendency to forget that we're looking through a frame at all!"

The Young Manager looked thoughtful. "How about a practical example?" he asked.

"Of course," said Gary. He crouched down beside a stack of framed pictures that were leaning against his work-bench. Carefully, he filed through them with his fingertips, picking out a small black and white print of an unusual aircraft.

"Take a look at this," he continued, laying the print down on the table and polishing the glass with his sleeve. "Back in 1959, an American industrialist offered a sizeable cash prize to the first team who could fly a human-powered aircraft over a one-mile course. Several well-funded outfits accepted the challenge, but despite their best efforts, the prize went unclaimed for nearly two decades. Until, that is, a team of engineers took a mental step back, and realised that the problem as the other teams were viewing it had been framed all wrong."

"How so?" asked the Young Manager, intrigued.

"They realised that the other teams were spending all of their time designing and building beautiful light-weight prototypes, trying to design the perfect solution. Sadly, this approach failed when each labour of love was destroyed when they crashed on their first test flight. It was back to square one with every fresh attempt."

"More time and money," the Young Manager added.

"Exactly," said Gary, "the eventual winners were the team who realised that they didn't need to design an aircraft that could fly the course first time. That was the wrong frame to view the problem through. What they needed was to design an aircraft that could survive crashing relatively intact. A solid base that they could build on, without going right back to basics every time. They focussed on making their aircraft quick and easy to repair."

"Which meant more attempts at the mile, and a quicker turnaround between attempts. Brilliant," said the Young Manager, "Instead of building *a plane that could fly*, they needed to build *a plane that could crash.* That's what you call changing the frame!"

"Quite," said Gary, "That's an engineering example, but it applies more broadly. It shows how teams of people can easily become stuck when they view a problematic situation through a single frame."

"So, in essence, we need to be careful that we're not just seeing one side of the situation," said the Young Manager.

"Well, it's not quite that simple," Gary clarified. He continued, "When we fail to acknowledge the frame that we've placed around a problem, the point of view that we've taken, we slip into the assumption that our view of things is the only one that is valid or correct. We come to believe, with a sense of certainty, that we have access to the one, right way of defining what the problem really is. We see our own way of viewing the problem as totally objective and inarguable, and in doing so, we open ourselves up to what psychologists call *Confirmation Bias*. We hold tight to anyone and anything that confirms our preconceptions, and we dismiss that which contradicts or challenges our view of things, because it doesn't fit the frame we're busy pretending isn't there. Are you with me?"

"I'd never thought of *people problems* in those terms. That's what I'm struggling with myself: group dynamics," mused the Young Manager, "But I have noticed that once someone labels an individual or group *challenging* or *difficult*, they rarely lose the label. I guess that's the frame getting in the way of progress."

"Precisely." Gary beamed. "If we need to deal with someone we consider to be argumentative, we'll tend to interpret everything they say and do from the moment that judgement is made through a frame that reinforces that assumption. If at any time they happen to disagree with us, that just confirms their argumentative character, right? And on the days when they're quite happy to go along with us, well…" Gary winked and said, "We can just ignore those, can't we, because they don't fit the frame. The truth is, there are many ways to frame problems, and there isn't generally one *right* frame for a specific problem."

"So how do we know which frame to look through?" asked the Young Manager.

"A process of elimination," Gary replied, "There may not be a *right* frame, but there's sure as Hell a *wrong* one! Remember this. It builds on what our friend has told you…"

We know someone is looking through the wrong frame whenever they find themselves pig wrestling.

"Let me get this straight in my own mind," the Young Manager said, slowly, "When someone ends up pig wrestling and is unable to create the change they need, that means they've got the wrong frame around their problem. That they're tackling the wrong problem."

"Exactly," said Gary, "If we find ourselves stuck in the mud, it's a dead cert that the old frame round that pig's neck is doing nothing to reveal the situation to us. It's time for a *new* frame."

The Young Manager nodded as he reflected on Gary's words. "So, how do you go about choosing a *new* frame?" he asked.

Gary waved a long-fingered hand dismissively. "The important thing," he said, "Is merely realising that the old frame has to go. That how you've framed the problem so far, or your perception of what kind of problem you thought you were tackling, needs to change. That's your starting point…"

We become immensely powerful when we decide that we will choose the frames through which we will view the world.

"And I suppose," the Young Manager said as he mused, "The more flexible you are with your view of a situation, the more options you have at your disposal."

"That's exactly right," said Gary, "Because we don't yet know which frame will provide the most effective way to view the problem, the one that will generate new insights or opportunities, we need to be able to try a series of different frames, until we find the right one. That takes flexible thinking."

He rifled through the stack of frames by his side, and pulled out another photograph: a panoramic view of Times Square at night, still buzzing with crowds, and bathed in the glow of its famous advertising signage.

"It's a nice shot, isn't it," he said, as the Young Manager leaned over the photograph, examining it closely, "But it's only one way of capturing the scene."

He pointed to a yellow cab, idling at the kerb.

"Through the frame of that cab driver's eyes, for example, you could tell a whole other story. Or here…" He pointed at a small crowd of people spilling up the steps from a basement bar. "Zoom in on those guys and the story's different again. But it doesn't end there. Pull in closer to *really* look at the expressions on their face, their body language, the dynamics of the crowd…you see what I mean? We could go on, picking out individual elements of the greater scene, and analysing their place in the whole, from dawn till dusk. All of that information is available to us when we examine the bigger picture in closer detail."

"It could go on forever!" exclaimed the Young Manager.

"And every picture-within-a-picture would tell a different story, even though they were part of the greater whole." Gary slipped the photograph back into the pile and leaned in towards his eager audience. "So let's get back to thinking about your situation."

"Please, yes," said the Young Manager.

"So," Gary began. "As we've established, in framing a situation, we make decisions about the information that we consider to be relevant. That's inevitable, whether by choice or chance. So if we want to identify new ways of solving our problems"—Gary tapped his forehead—"we need to switch our thinking and get creative. And any successful creative endeavour involves shifting one's frame of reference to incorporate details you might ordinarily have missed…"

> **Any breakthrough in thinking about a problem situation involves a change to the frame that's around the pig's neck.**

The Young Manager scrolled through his notes. "I need to summarise this for myself," he said, tracing his bullet points with his tablet's stylus:

SUMMARY

- If you find yourself pig wrestling, then you're looking through the wrong frame.
- Your power increases immensely when you take control of the frames through which you choose to view the world.
- The first breakthrough in any problem-solving situation is the realisation that the frame needs to change.

"Nicely put," said Gary, smiling, "Recognising that we can reframe our problems, viewing and describing them differently is fundamental to Problem Cleaning. But to find a better frame for a problem, we'll need to clean our thinking *and* the language that we use to express it," he added, "And that, my new friend, brings us to the next element of the Pig Pen scene."

RED BUCKET AND SPONGE

"Dealing with a clean pig is one thing," said Gary, leaning on his bony elbows, "That would be tough enough. But our pigs aren't clean, are they? They're caked with mud from the pig pen. Why, you can hardly see what they are at all!"

"What are you getting at?" asked the Young Manager.

"Well, how about I give you another example, " Gary replied. "It might help demonstrate the need to clean your thinking, if you really want to create the changes that you need."

"That would be great," said the Young Manager, tapping his tablet to begin a new section of notes.

"Back when we first started exploring Problem Cleaning as a process," Gary began, "we heard about a problem that the authorities of an Amsterdam airport were wrestling with. You see, the conditions of the men's-room urinals were a little unpleasant to say the least, and certainly not in line with the kind of welcome that the airport wanted to create. Added to which, the costs of keeping the floors clean were becoming increasingly expensive."

"That certainly sounds like a messy problem," quipped the Young Manager, looking up from his tablet.

"Right," Gary said, smiling. "So in trying to change the behaviour of the men who used the facilities, the airport authorities initially tried the obvious solution. Implicitly framing the situation as a 'health education problem', they placed signs above each urinal politely reminding the men of the need to keep the facilities hygienic for the benefit of everyone."

The Young Manager looked doubtful. "I'm guessing that made little difference?"

"None whatsoever. Because let's be honest, even the most educated men amongst us sometimes make mistakes don't we," Gary said with a wink. "When we heard about that attempted solution, we wondered if their next step might have involved trying to motivate the users to take more care. Perhaps they'd tried appealing to a sense of pride about the environment and the facilities, linking it to the first experience of the city, or something similar.

"Anyway, to cut a long story short," he went on, "whatever they tried, none of it led to any kind of lasting change. The urinals were just as unhygienic as they'd always been."

"So what did they do?" asked the Young Manager.

"Well, it was at that point that they took a mental step back and thought differently. They identified someone who could etch into porcelain and had them engrave an image of a single black housefly into the bowl of each of the urinals."

"And why did they do *that*," asked the Young Manager.

"They did *that* because they'd cleaned the problem," Gary replied. "Put simply, they recognised that they didn't have an *education* or a *motivation* problem. That was just dirty thinking. Taking the time to clean their thinking and their language, they realised what they actually had was an *aiming problem*. As soon as the men were given a target to aim for, in this case a single black housefly, spillage was immediately reduced by eighty percent, and the cleaning costs fell dramatically."

"That's brilliant!" exclaimed the Young Manager. "It's such a neat solution."

"It is," replied Gary, "but it only becomes a possibility once the problem is *clean*. It could have been so tempting for the authorities to continue tackling a 'health education' problem, or a 'motivation' problem, even if their solutions would never deliver the results that they needed."

The Young Manager nodded as he reflected on the story, "I think I see what you mean. So you're saying that we need to clean our language and our thinking so we can create the change that's really needed?"

"Precisely," said Gary, "The mud represents our dirty thinking, and that dirty thinking is reflected in the language we use, and the assumptions we make, about our problems. As long as you're getting covered in the dirt, and not grasping the real problem underneath, you'll be stuck pig wrestling forever. You can start to tackle that impasse, though, by recognising that, in the first place, it's not your fault. These biases in your thinking and limitations in your language are inherited. You played no part in their establishment. But you're here now, right? So it's your responsibility to be aware of the muddiness of your thinking—of cultural bias or inherited assumptions—and to safeguard against them.

"The problems we wrestle with," Gary added, sagely, "And the frames through which we see them, are shaped and reinforced by the stories that we tell ourselves. In fact," he summarised…

The way we describe a problem to ourselves is often the core factor keeping that problem firmly in place.

"I've never really considered the power of language in that way," the Young Manager commented.

"Its power is immense," said Gary. "We humans have an overriding desire to describe and explain the situations that we face. But we're not generally very good at describing those same situations *accurately*," said Gary. "Our stories are heavily edited and assembled to fit our own world views. They're full of assumptions, information gaps, and sloppy language. But, of course, because we formulate them ourselves, we cannot help but think that they are true…"

When you find yourself pig wrestling, it's the labels, stories and assumptions that you have applied to the situation that are truly holding you stuck.

The Young Manager furrowed his brow, thinking back over the times when he'd built his approach on second-hand accounts of different situations. "I guess sometimes it's just easier to accept someone else's version of events," asked the Young Manager. "Then *that* becomes the frame through which your own investigation is seen."

"Unfortunately, yes," Gary agreed. "Sometimes the least useful thing you can ask for is someone else's summary of a situation. I'm sure you'll have heard these words before: *What we need here is better communication.*"

"Countless times," groaned the Young Manager agreeing. "And half of them from me!"

Gary burst out laughing. "Well then"—he chuckled—"I'm sure you'll also have noticed that when you say it, most people sit and nod sagely like they've got an audience with a prophet. But if you were to ask the question, *How, specifically, could we communicate better?* you'd be sitting in silence, right?"

This time, it was the Young Manager's turn to chuckle. "So you're telling me that vague statements like *we need better communication* are just sops. Simple labels that everyone can agree on, but which get us nowhere."

"That's right," Gary said and nodded. "They don't move things forward in any way. But the point I really want to make is that…"

We must take control of the stories we tell and the descriptions we apply to our lives, or they will take control of us.

The Young Manager was quiet for a moment. "I've heard it said that there is no more powerful story told than the one we tell ourselves."

Gary smiled and said, "You know, I really believe that to be true."

"So when I find myself struggling to create the change that I need, I need to be especially aware of the narrative that I'm applying to the situation," said the Young Manager.

"Precisely," said Gary. "When someone tells us one story—one version of events—we often begin from a position of healthy scepticism. We, quite reasonably, question the authority and intentions of the person relating it to us. But when the person telling us the story is *us*, we rarely apply the same rigour. We don't question our own authority or intentions. We take our own word for it, if you like. And that's a shame, because when it comes to explaining situations, some of our most basic biases come into play. We fall foul of thinking traps like the *Fundamental Attribution Error*."

"The Fundamental what?" asked the Young Manager, raising an eyebrow.

"It's a term from psychology," Gary explained. "The *Fundamental Attribution Error* is what happens when we observe someone performing an isolated behaviour, and are too quick to generalise about our observation. Instead of seeing it in isolation, we assume that it is representative of a longstanding, predictable, stable character trait. And from the moment of that error, for evermore, we view the other person through the frame of our initial error."

"This I know about," said the Young Manager. "Just the other day we had an inter-departmental meeting and one of my team left an empty coffee cup on the meeting room table. All hell broke loose after he'd left the room. Well," he clarified, "a sort of passive-aggressive Hell, but you get the picture. It's company policy to clean up after yourself, so everyone was moaning about how 'untidy' and 'lazy' the culprit was. Thing is, I saw him yesterday and I didn't think about the fantastic report he prepared for me last month, or the fact that he's beating his targets every quarter. I just thought, *Oh look, there's the messy guy who can't pick up his coffee cup*. Now I realise that I messed up when the gossip was flying. I should have nipped it in the bud. Who knows why he left his cup on the table. Preoccupied? Absent-minded? Who even cares. It's not like he does it at every meeting, but *already* I was allowing myself to see this employee through an ill-fitting and, frankly, unjust frame!"

"Now you're getting it!" Gary smiled. "But it doesn't end there. We have a terrible habit of making judgements about people's capabilities based on very little actual evidence. At the Collective we sometimes call this one the *Capability Assessment Error*."

"You're going to have to flesh that out for me too," said the Young Manager, glancing up from his furious note taking.

"Okay," said Gary, "for example, you take a simple behaviour like *remaining quiet in team meetings*, and you label it as a *lack of leadership potential*. A semiaccurate description of a behaviour is taken as evidence of a deficiency of skills. But there's really no reason to believe that the former affects the latter. That sort of muddy thinking lies at the heart of a lot of workplace people problems."

"And I know from experience," the Young Manager offered, "that those labels stick."

"Like mud," Gary replied.

"So how do I avoid these pitfalls?" asked the Young Manager.

"With your bucket and sponge," said Gary, matter-of-factly. "Scrub away the mud of your dirty thinking. Being aware of it is half the problem solved already, so all you need do is…"

Take the time to accurately describe the problem in behavioural and factual terms, rather than prematurely applying meaning and labels.

"Ideally," Gary continued, "you need to describe the mechanics of the problem in concrete factual terms. Lay it out in such a way that no-one can argue with the validity of your account. Whenever you wrestle with a problem, you need to notice your dirty thinking patterns, and take a moment to clean things up. A clean pig is a happier prospect already. And once you've got that porker all pink and shiny, you'll have a better idea of what frame would look best around his neck, too."

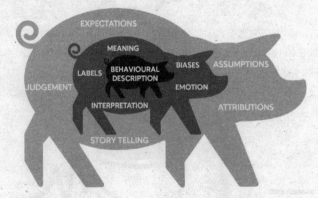

The Young Manager fell silent, considering what he'd just heard. "So, in a nutshell, I must be aware of this dirty thinking when I'm struggling to create change," he spoke almost to himself, scrolling through the notes on his screen. He looked up frowning. "But all these assumptions, labels and meanings that we apply to problems are pretty hard to shed, aren't they?"

"They are," Gary replied. "But the only way to move forward is to clean up your thinking. But beware," he warned, "If you're helping someone else to clean their thinking, you need to take great care. Our language typically only stresses one side of an interaction, helping people to see other sides needs to be done with care. In negotiating the removal of a frame that has been around a situation for some time, we need to gently challenge the language, assumptions and stories that lie behind it."

"We're essentially looking for the hard facts, but doing so with soft touches," the Young Manager reflected.

"You know, that's a really nice turn of phrase," Gary said with a smile. "No-one will thank you for snatching their frame and smashing it in front of a crowded room. Instead, we need to calmly unearth the inarguable facts of the situation, to go slowly, and to take care."

"There's certainly a lot to consider here," said the Young Manager. "Let me make sure I've understood correctly…"

SUMMARY

- The descriptions and narratives we apply to our problems are often linked to our failure to make progress.
- When you're pig wrestling, the labels, stories, and assumptions you apply to the situation are the mud that the pig is stuck in!
- You have to take control of the narrative you apply to life, or it will control you.
- Take the time to accurately describe a problem in behavioural and factual terms. Never accept the labels and assumptions that come with a situation.

"That captures it all rather nicely, I think," said Gary, smiling.

"Thanks," replied the Young Manager. "It makes total sense."

"I'm glad you agree," Gary nodded. He tilted his head to one side, regarding the Young Manager, kindly. "You know, I think you're ready to move on to the next part of the Pig Pen."

"Okay, fire away," said the Young manager, stylus poised.

But Gary stood up, scraping the legs of his stool on the hardwood floor.

"Not my area." He smiled. "Time for you to meet another member of our little gang of problem cleaners."

He took a business card from his pocket and handed it to the Young Manager. It read:

Kate Hamilton
Out of the Box Marketing
Unit 20—The Collective

"You'll find her on the top floor," said Gary, pointing a long, elegant finger at the ceiling.

The Young Manager stood and took Gary's hand, shaking it warmly as he thanked him for his time.

"Welcome to life outside the pig pen!" Gary called out behind him as he made for the stairs.

As he walked, the Young Manager's thoughts turned to some of the problems he'd found himself wrestling with recently. How often had he wholeheartedly bought into the careless labelling of a situation, he wondered? He knew he was guilty of jumping ahead to action on occasion, without so much as a moment to consider his own dirty thinking. His staff engagement problem was a case in point. Based on their survey scores, the leadership team had quickly slipped a frame around the problem, and ploughed head first into all sorts of erroneous assumptions. Emotive language had been used, threatening stories had been told, and little or no time had been spent on unearthing the hard facts behind the abstract data. The Young Manager had been party to these discussions, and had found himself wrestling with this ill-defined problem in the early hours. As he reached the bottom of the stairs, he voiced his thoughts to himself, aloud.

"If I find myself pig wrestling," he muttered, as he took the bannister, "then I know for sure I've got the wrong frame around the problem. So how else can I frame this engagement problem, because that frame is definitely keeping us stuck?" He sighed wearily. "But if it's *not* an engagement problem, what kind of problem *is* it though?" The Young Manager reflected on the language that had been used to describe the problem and the labels that had definitely been prematurely applied. They had to strip it all down to a factual description, but what were the facts?

The Young Manager resolved to ask these very questions of the leadership team, the next time he met with them. He'd also make sure to challenge any of the dirty thinking and labels that the team were getting stuck on. As he began to climb the staircase he recalled what he had learnt.

Step-by-step, in his mind's eye he walked through the scene he had memorised, from the lush green field, to the pig pen. Mentally, he placed one foot on the bottom board of the fence—a moment to check how specifically was it a problem for him, if he'd seen the whites of its eyes, and whether the timing was right…then he peered into the pen. Saw the pig, wedged into its picture frame—a reminder to think about the frame through which his problems were viewed…saw the mud and the bucket and sponge—representative of the muddy thinking that holds back progress, and the steps that need to be taken to clean things up…

He nodded to himself, satisfied that he had recalled all of the key elements of the scene correctly. And, as he did so, he reached the highest floor of the building.

Kate Hamilton stood at the top of the stairs, waiting for him.

SOLUTIONEERING

Kate Hamilton, a petite woman of about five foot three, who exuded quiet authority like a plutonium rod giving off radiation, held out her hand for the Young Manager to shake and smiled warmly. Her blue-eyed gaze was direct and unwavering.

"Gary texted ahead," she said brightly. "It sounds as though you've had a busy morning. I imagine your head's spinning somewhat, is it?"

"Right on both counts," the Young Manager admitted, grinning.

"Well, don't worry," said Kate. "It will all fit together and make sense soon enough." She led him briskly down the corridor, talking as they went. "Adopting a different way of looking at challenging situations takes time, but once you've got your head around it, the process becomes intuitive."

At the end of the corridor, Kate pushed open a set of double doors and led the Young Manager into a large, busy, open plan office. It was a colourful, space, designed to encourage a playful attitude. Primary coloured freestanding meeting pods dotted the room and one corner was given over to leather bean bags, games consoles and a well-used office ping-pong table. Some worked from standing desks, while others chatted and shared notes as they lounged on sofas with their tablets and laptops. One or two people had treadmills attached to their desks so they could walk while they worked.

"We let the staff design their own workstations. It does wonders for productivity." said Kate, noticing the Young Manager's wide eyes. "Jelly bean?" she asked, as they passed a spherical glass candy dispenser on a bright red metal stand.

"I'm fine, thanks," said the Young Manager, holding up a palm.

Kate ushered him into one of the meeting pods and pulled the frosted screen across the entrance to muffle the sound of her busy team. A trestle table ran up the middle of the space with picnic benches arranged on either side. Kate gestured to one of the benches. "Make yourself comfortable," she said, glancing at her watch. "I've got a new copy-writer turning up in an hour, but we should be done well before then."

"Thanks," said the Young Manager, "for your time, I mean."

Kate nodded as she slid onto the opposite bench. She arranged a small pile of papers in front of herself then, without further ado, she launched into a conversation that seemed like a polished presentation after Gary's relaxed chat.

TIN FEEDING TROUGH

"I'm going to dive straight in with how the Feeding Trough can create breakthroughs in your thinking, as well as how it can help you to spot the assumptions that are holding you back. So, what's in the trough, eh? What have you been feeding this problem pig of yours?"

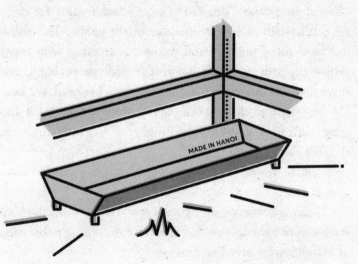

"Rage and frustration mostly." said the Young Manager.

"I can imagine." Kate smiled. "Okay. First stop, French Hanoi, 1902. The city's colonial authorities had a pig of their own to wrestle…"

The Young Manager fired up his tablet and began a new section of notes.

"Hanoi was infested with rats." Kate continued, without pausing for breath, "We're talking Pied Piper levels. Biblical plague levels. And nothing the city's bosses tried was having an impact. They couldn't recruit enough rat catchers. They were completely overrun. So, in desperation, they switched strategy. Instead of hiring yet more pest control workers, the colonial government decided to offer a cash bounty for every rat pelt handed in by any member of the public. The policy was announced publicly and received favourably, with many people expecting a quick end to the city's rat problem. But that's not how things worked out." Shaking her head, she said, "In fact, far from clearing out the rats, things soon took a dramatic turn for the worse. The number of rats in Hanoi went through the roof!"

"I don't get it," said the Young Manager, puzzled. "How come?"

"I thought you might figure it out"—Kate winked, miming a wad of banknotes—"because the enterprising population of Hanoi started breeding rats."

The Young Manager burst out laughing. "Of course they did!" he said, feeling foolish for having missed the obvious scam. He let his laughter subside before adding "Forgive me, though. I don't see how your story helps me."

Kate raised an eyebrow and fixed him with her steel gaze. "Think about it," she said. "The solution that the authorities came up with tells us a lot about how they framed their problem. Based on their strategy, they framed the situation as being one where they needed to *increase the number of dead rats*."

"What!?" said the Young Manager. "But wasn't that the problem they were trying to tackle?"

"Not quite," Kate replied. "Whilst that might seem to make sense, it is the wrong frame. A better frame would have been to *decrease the number of living rats*. That is a very different problem." Kate tapped a finger on the table and said, "So you see, when you have the wrong frame around a problem…"

Our misguided attempts at resolving problems can often fuel the real problem.

"So, if choosing the wrong frame can have such a disastrous impact," the Young Manager asked, "how do I find the right one?"

"I'm glad you asked," said Kate, "because I've been playing with the photocopier." She pushed a pile of paper over to the Young Manager's side of the table, keeping a single sheet back for herself. "How about a little practical experiment?" she asked him.

The Young Manager leafed through the top few pages of the pile, noting the same pattern of nine dots arranged in a three-by-three square, printed on each page.

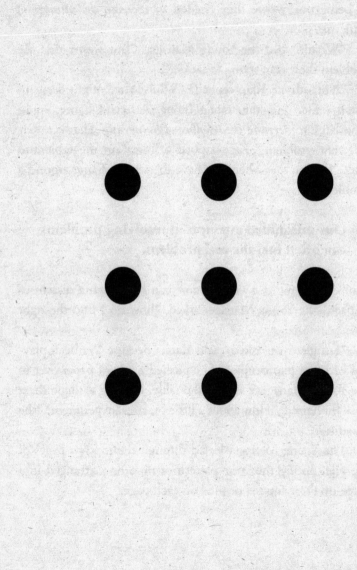

Kate handed the Young Manager a marker pen. "I want you to connect these nine dots, using four straight lines, but without taking your pen off the page."

"No problem!" declared the Young Manager, confidently. He'd seen this puzzle somewhere before—on a training course, perhaps, or at a conference. As he placed the pen firmly on the top left dot, though, he faltered, and with a sinking feeling, he realised that he couldn't actually remember the answer.

"Have as many goes as you like," said Kate, mischievously, indicating the sizeable stack of copies that she had provided.

"I'll get it," said the Young Manager, screwing up his second attempt and reaching for a third sheet. "I just need to remember the trick. Damn!" He scribbled over his latest attempt and frowned.

For all his best efforts, the Young Manager couldn't crack Kate's problem. He could feel the pressure was mounting with each failed attempt. The meeting pod was slowly filling up with crumpled sheets, as the stack of fresh ones shrunk smaller and smaller. It was positively embarrassing!

"I think you've suffered enough," said Kate, after a while. "Shall we take a look at the solution together?"

The Young Manager blew the air from his cheeks and set down his pen with relief. "I think we better had," he said, grinning sheepishly.

Kate turned over the single sheet that she had reserved, to reveal the puzzle's answer.

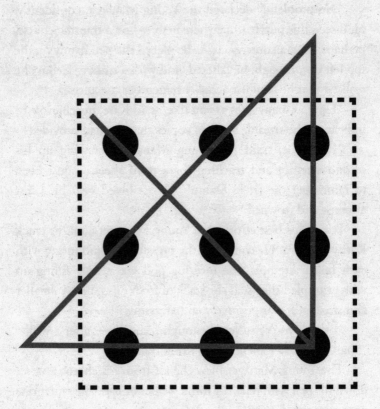

"Of course!" exclaimed the Young Manager, slapping his forehead melodramatically. "You've got to think outside the box, as we've all heard a million times. Look beyond the grid of dots and go *beyond* the lines they form."

"Actually, that's not quite right," said Kate. "What we're saying is that if you hold that assumption, you make it an unsolvable problem. Once you realise that you're making those assumptions, the potential solutions become endless," said Kate. "Do you see how you effectively penned in your own thinking with that single assumption you made about the rules of the game?"

"I do now," said the Young Manager ruefully, "but when you're stuck in the rut, it's not so easy."

"That's normal," Kate replied. "But by exploring what hasn't worked, we can sometimes find the key to unlocking a problematic situation."

"If it doesn't work, try something else," added the Young Manager.

"Exactly," Kate answered, "but try to remember that it is possible to convince yourself that you are trying all kinds of new angles, when in reality, you may be locked into variations of the same failed approach."

"Okay, I get that, but how does it relate to the people problems I've been facing?" asked the Young Manager.

"Let me give you an example," Kate began. "Whenever we ask someone with a problem what they've already tried, their answer is always roughly the same."

"It is?" asked the Young Manager, incredulously. "Enlighten me."

"Well, they always say that they've *tried everything*," Kate replied, "but that's rarely the whole truth of the matter."

"I've said it myself, a thousand times!" the Young Manager admitted. "But it was always said with sincerity. Only when I really *had* exhausted my options."

Kate looked doubtful. "Well I'm sure you felt like you had tried everything," she said, "just like you felt like you'd tried everything with those nine dots. That is, until you realised that there was a whole other world of options available to you if you didn't make the assumption and stick within the imaginary lines. But"—she held up a finger, emphatically—"what's really fascinating is that in these failed attempts lies the key to real progress. Because, while we may legitimately *feel* like we have tried everything, we're often only working within a small subset of potential solutions."

"But how do these failed attempts point to the *right* solution?" asked the Young Manager, glancing at the pile of crumpled puzzle sheets. "Even if you'd pointed out straight away that I was making an assumption that was preventing me from seeing the solution, I'm not sure I'd have been able to identify that assumption myself."

"Fair enough," said Kate. "It's not always easy to spot where you're going wrong. But, let's take another look at some of your failed attempts," she suggested. "Lay them out on the table in front of you so we can see them all together. Go on…"

Kate pointed at the crumpled papers that littered the pod. The Young Manager raised his eyebrows in query, and she nodded. He took one of the screwed up sheets and carefully opened it out, flattening it out on the table. Then he did the same for another, and another, laying them all out together, so that they covered the table.

"So," said Kate, when there was no room left for any more puzzle sheets, "do you see what they all have in common?"

"Like we said," the Young Manager replied, "the obvious thing is that I stayed within an imaginary box with every attempt. I assumed that not going beyond the grid was part of the rules of the game, but in truth, nobody ever told me that."

"That's right," Kate said and nodded. "That's the assumption that held your thinking captive. And until you spotted that, you were going to be stuck feeling as though you'd *tried everything*."

"True," agreed the Young Manager.

"And in a sense you had," Kate agreed. "But only everything within that narrow frame you'd given yourself. Now that the full picture is laid out before you, it's obvious"—she indicated the table covered in failed puzzles—"Your mind is open now. But tell me, what else do your attempts have in common?"

"Hmm," said the Young Manager, thinking hard, "I used the same pen for all of them, I suppose…"

"Yes, you did," Kate replied. "But who said you had to stick to the pen I gave you? In theory, you could have found a pen with a nib thick enough to connect the dots with a single pen stroke."

"I could have thought about folding the paper too, maybe," said the Young Manager. "Look at me," he added self-effacingly. "I'm on a roll now."

"Good thinking," said Kate. "Do you see how getting an overview of our failed attempts, can help identify the assumptions that are holding us back, and open our minds to new solutions? In essence…"

The themes that connect our failed attempts to resolve a problem highlight the assumptions we are making.

"Those assumptions might be driven by personal experience or misapplied knowledge," Kate suggested, "or by entrenched cultural notions concerning how we should go about creating change."

"Like the strategies for dealing with difficult people that my colleagues suggested, you mean?" asked the Young Manager. "All of which were about educating or motivating the staff in one way or another." He rolled his eyes. "As if we haven't been *there* before!"

"Exactly like that," said Kate, gathering up the papers again into a neat pile. "Even changing something as simple as the context, or the location of where you attempt your solutions can help. So many solutions to people problems are only ever attempted in a formal, business environment. You'd be surprised by the number of problems that get resolved when the context changes, am I right?" She indicated the playful open plan space beyond the meeting pod.

"I take your point," said the Young Manager, thoughtfully. "So are there other ways to identify assumptions and potential solutions?"

"Well, here's another way to think about your previous attempts that didn't quite crack the problem," said Kate. "Consider the times where you tried something that had a positive impact on the problem, but the impact did not last. Now ask yourself two things: *What part of those solutions really seemed to work?* and *What stopped you from doing more of this approach?* Run through those questions and you'll soon have a new frame to try out.

"Alternatively," she went on, "you could look at those attempted solutions that made the problem measurably worse, and consider what performing the *opposite* of those actions might entail. Just like the people of Hanoi, to bring things back to my earlier story."

"I'd never thought that my failed attempts contained so much useful information," said the Young Manager. "When I try something that totally bombs, I tend to tick it off the list, sweep it under the carpet and forget all about it."

"And it's precisely that tendency that holds you back from resolving challenging problems," Kate said, decisively. "Maintain your critical eye. Look at unsuccessful solutions.

Engage with your failures to open up new ways of thinking, and find new frames to look through."

A sudden knock on the pod's frosted door made them both jump. The glass slid open to reveal a stout little man in his forties, with an anxious look on his round face. He had a shiny bald head and a thick bushy moustache. An equally stout French Bulldog wearing a diamante collar stood at his feet staring up at him adoringly, and panting noisily. Kate beckoned him in, and man and dog made their way inside to stand at the foot of the rough wooden table.

"I'm sorry to disturb you," the man said briskly, "but our guest has arrived rather early, Kate. What do you want me to do with him?"

Kate glanced at her watch. "Sort him out with something to drink and a biscuit, will you, Julian? I'll be over soon."

The man nodded, reversed out of the pod, and bustled off across the office, with his dog at his heels.

"Actually," said Kate, watching her employee leave, "Julian is a pretty good case study for what I was just talking about."

"How so?" asked the Young Manager.

"A year ago, his performance had slipped to the point where I was genuinely thinking about letting him go." Kate pulled a face and sighed, heavily. "I didn't want it to come to that, of course. Julian's been with me for years, and he's enormously talented. A real asset when he's on form. It was the pig wrestling method that helped me to see his fall in performance through a different frame. And when I did that, I learnt something. I found out that the problem wasn't with Julian at all; it was with Doris."

"Doris?" asked the Young Manager.

"Doris the bulldog," said Kate, laughing. "To cut a long story short, Julian started coming into the office late and sneaking off early at the end of the day. He was distracted and unfocused and stopped meeting deadlines." She frowned. "I had to do something to shake things up, so I scheduled early morning briefings, to force him to come in on time."

"Did that work at all?" asked the Young Manager.

"Total disaster!" said Kate. "He got here on time, but was more distracted than ever and then nipped off even earlier at the end of the day. A real rats of Hanoi moment."

"So what did you do?"

"Played hardball," Kate replied. "I scheduled our team meetings for the end of the day, so he couldn't wriggle out of his designated office hours." She rolled her eyes. "That was a mistake. Julian started getting very stressed and snappy with everyone. The whole thing became unbearable for us all. It wasn't until I looked at all the things I had tried that I realised where I'd gone wrong. Everything had been about trying to keep Julian at work and away from home. Working from home simply isn't an option in his role, so I had to consider something else entirely. I wondered if rather than keeping him away from whatever was requiring so much attention at home, maybe we should do the opposite and bring that thing into work." She smiled. "It turned out the thing was Doris. Julian had assumed that there was no way we could have a bulldog around the place, so he never asked."

"What was up with Doris?" asked the Young Manager.

"She'd started pining badly for Julian while they were apart. It was affecting her health, not to mention his soft furnishings. And it was distracting him from his work on a daily basis. So now Doris comes to work *with* him, and Julian is firing on all cylinders again. It was as simple as that. Having an office dog around the place has done wonders for other people's stress levels too. And our clients love her. It all worked out rather well."

"I wouldn't mind an office dog myself," said the Young Manager wistfully. He sat forward on his bench, making as if to rise. "I'm sure I shouldn't take up any more of your time. I don't want you to keep anyone waiting on my account," he said.

"Don't worry," said Kate, stopping him from getting up with a wave of her hand. "I've got exactly enough time to show you the next element of the pig-pen mnemonic. And you don't want to miss this part. It's my favourite way to step outside of those assumptions that you're making."

CRYSTAL BALL

"The problem with problems in general," Kate said, continuing her tutorial, "is that we spend far too much time and effort trying to figure out what we should do to solve them."

The Young Manager looked puzzled. "And, trying to solve problems is a problem?"

"It can be," said Kate, "because most people spend too much time thinking about how to solve the problem, and not enough time on figuring out how they'd know if the problem were solved. To get around that, the pig-pen crowd use something called the *Miracle Question*."

"Well, it'll take a miracle to resolve my work problems, so fire away," said the Young Manager, drily.

"The Miracle Question," said Kate, ignoring his joke, "is an exercise that focuses on ensuring that we know exactly what we're trying to achieve when we set out to effect change."

"Shouldn't that be obvious?" asked the Young Manager.

"You'd be surprised," said Kate. "The Miracle Question allows you to explore the outcome you genuinely need, not what you *think* you need, by looking past obstacles and focusing on possibilities for the future."

"Possibilities for the future…" repeated the Young Manager, making a note on his tablet.

Kate nodded. She pressed her fingertips together and leaned across the table. "The questions that we ask define our reality. They can help us to live our *best life*, or they can derail us completely. The genius behind the Miracle Question is that it forces you to stop thinking about how you might solve a problem, and instead focus on how you'd know it was solved. Picture perfection, then work back from there, to identify what you really need happen."

"That actually sounds pretty simple," said the Young Manager. "I'm great with *what ifs*."

"It might sound simple, but that doesn't mean it's easy," said Kate. "Most people can rattle off the problems in their life easily enough, but they often struggle when it comes to answering the Miracle Question. The miracle question isn't about finding solutions, it's about how you'd know the solution had been found and implemented successfully. It bypasses the need to find a solution and so helps people avoid getting stuck in searching for the solution. The crucial point is that you have to…"

Stop thinking about how you are going to solve this problem, and start thinking how you'll know it is solved.

"Fine," said the Young Manager, "tell me how to do that, then."

Kate reached into her pocket for a piece of neatly folded paper. She unfolded it to reveal a printed picture of the crystal ball from the pig-pen scene, and pushed it across the table to the Young Manager.

"I didn't have a real one to hand, I'm afraid," she joked. "So we'll have to make do with my photocopying skills again. Take a moment to…"

Imagine that you could look into this crystal ball, to a time after a miracle had happened. What would you see once this problem was solved?

"Now, examine that picture closely. Filter out the *nice-to-haves*, and identify the *need-to-haves*. The things that will need to have changed to accomplish your vision. Go on. Give me a couple of examples."

The Young Manager thought for a few moments. "Okay," he said finally, "so if there's been a miracle…the teams that I manage have stopped disagreeing and started getting along with each other. Oh, and the challenging people in those teams have got into the habit of automatically updating the monthly spreadsheet with their data, without constantly needing to be nagged."

"Well," said Kate, "that's an interesting place to start. In the first place, both of those descriptions are crammed full of dirty language and generalisations. And secondly they both sound like solutions pretending to be problems."

The Young Manager was annoyed with himself. He'd made exactly the error that Gary had warned him about. "Busted," he said sheepishly. "I should have been thinking about facts and behaviours rather than generalising. But what do you mean by *solutions pretending to be problems*?"

"Let's look at the second part of the miracle you painted," Kate continued. "I'm guessing that what you actually *need* is a regular and reliable source of numbers from your people, so you can collate them into a single file. I'm guessing your *monthly spreadsheet* is the current means of gathering that data, right?"

"Right," said the Young Manager, still unsure of the point Kate was making.

Kate smiled. "That monthly spreadsheet of yours isn't one of your problems at all. It's a failed solution to the problem of data gathering. There are many other ways to collate that data without using a group spreadsheet and touring the office to nag your staff. At the end of the day, all you need are the figures. Try a phone call, or a regular round of coffees with a data catch-up. Maybe you could solve the problem simply by delegating that data gathering to a junior member of the team, for whom it would be higher up their own list of priorities. It depends on what you are trying to achieve. Just make sure you stay focussed on the *need-to-haves,* not the *nice-to-haves.* Sure, it would be lovely if every one of your employees were conscientious and proactive in updating spreadsheets. But they're not. The notion that you can encourage them towards perfection in this regard is a Utopian fallacy, a road that leads to lifelong pig wrestling and frustration."

"I think I know what you mean," the Young Manager replied, slightly defensively. "But is it really too much to ask that the staff just email their results to me? Isn't it disrespectful of them to ignore my request?"

"Oh, I see," said Kate, with a sideways smile. "So the problem *isn't* the numbers. It's that you don't feel you're getting the respect you deserve."

"Well, no, not really…I mean, it *is* the numbers"—the Young Manager blushed—"only it would be nice if—"

"I'm going to stop you there," Kate cut in. "It would be *nice* if your staff showed unswerving respect for your authority, and it would be *nice* if they did everything you ever asked without question or carelessness. But that's not a particularly realistic expectation, is it?"

"I guess not," the Young Manager agreed.

"See?" said Kate. "Those *nice-to-haves* have lead you straight into a muddy pig pen and left you stuck there. The labels you're attaching to the people in your team are penning in your thinking. They're being *disrespectful* and *unreliable*. Moreover, getting hung up on the *nice-to-haves* is holding you back from seeing what the *need-to-haves* actually are."

"To be honest," the Young Manager reflected and said, "I can think of dozens of times when I've tried something that I pretty much knew wouldn't address the underlying issue, just to feel like I was doing *something*."

"Taking action for the sake of appearances," said Kate, "that's not uncommon. But fluffing around with the nonessentials while failing to address the fundamentals is a bit like putting lipstick on a pig isn't it?"

They both chuckled at the mental image.

"Switch your thinking," Kate continued, "and you'll be able to step outside of your assumptions to see the full range of solutions that are available to you."

The Young Manager scrolled through his notes. "Okay," he said, "let's summarise the Tin Feeding Trough, and the Crystal Ball…"

SUMMARY

- Our misguided attempts to solve a problem can feed and exacerbate the problem itself.
- The themes that connect our failed attempts highlight the assumptions that are holding us back.

- Stop thinking how you are going to solve this problem, and start thinking how you'll know it's solved.

- Imagine that you could look into this crystal ball to a time after a miracle had happened. What would you see once this problem was solved?

- Filter out the *nice-to-have*s, and focus on the *need-to-haves*.

"Not a bad summary," said Kate. "You've got the key point, which is to stop solutioneering for a moment, and look at what you've already tried. Spot the assumptions you're making and identify what you really need to happen instead. Both of those strategies will help you to spot the old frame that you've put around the problem, and identify a new frame that fits better."

"Thanks Kate," the Young Manager said. "I feel like I might be making real progress. You know, I think I maybe understand enough of this process to get cracking!"

"You're welcome, but take care," Kate warned. "Having learnt the first few elements, it can be tempting to think that you know enough to begin taking action. But that would be a mistake. What you'll learn next will ensure that you don't waste your own and everyone else's time. It will allow you to create the change you need, in an efficient and impactful way."

"Understood," the Young Manager replied, somewhat apologetically. "I guess I'm getting ahead of myself."

"That's only natural," Kate replied with a smile. "Now, speaking of being efficient, I'm going to have to cut things short, but we should meet for coffee and a chat soon."

"Definitely," said the Young Manager, grinning broadly, as he reached out to shake her hand, "I know just the place."

"Best espresso in the city," Kate said with a wink. "Now, two more stops and you can get on with your life," she added, leading them out of the meeting room. "David's next. He'll take you through the next three elements of the Pig Pen. He's a sport's coach by profession. Head down to the basement. They've got the whole level. I'll let him know you're on your way."

"In more ways than one, I hope," said the Young Manager.

"No doubt," said Kate encouragingly, before nodding a final farewell and walking briskly away.

The Young Manager left Kate's colourful top floor office and headed down to the basement. He took the stairs to give himself time to think about his troubles again. Now he knew that his assumptions had kept him trapped inside the pig pen, just like Kate had said. How often had he been guilty of trying variations on the same failed solution? He'd certainly never thought to look at what might connect all of those failed attempts. And what of his *people problem*? It seemed he had been looking through the wrong frame all along?

His mind wandered to thoughts of the firm's new IT system. It was intended to enhance collaboration, and so much time and money had been invested in its design and roll-out. Was that just a solution pretending to be a problem as Kate had suggested? Now he wondered why, by comparison, so little time had been spent identifying how the leadership team would know whether their staff *were* collaborating better. The sloppily designed collaborative practices might actually be feeding some of the problems they were aimed at resolving! The Young Manager's mind was filling with new questions—What did they specifically need to happen? How much collaboration was enough? Surely expecting everyone to collaborate on everything was one of those utopian fallacies, wasn't it? What were the *nice-to-haves* and the *need-to-haves*?

The Young Manager resolved to explore this in depth with the team when he got back to the office. The current solution was certainly throwing up more problems that it was solving.

MAPPING

A tracksuited David was waiting for the Young Manager in the foyer of the Basement Fitness Centre.

"Thanks for seeing me," said the Young Manager, marvelling at the space around him. It was a cavern of a place, flooded with light and activity. "I had no idea that all this was down here," he told David.

"It's a proper Tardis, isn't it?" David grinned and said, "Come on, let's go to my office so we can talk."

The large space at the entrance to the gym formed a central circulation area leading off to different rooms for weights, exercise machines, and classes. Glass walls divided the different areas, bright light filled every corner, and the air smelled faintly of fresh towels and muscle rubs. They walked past a large, glass-fronted gym, full of people sweating their way through circuit training, and the Young Manager sucked in his stomach and vowed to renew his own gym membership.

"What sport do you coach, then?" asked the Young Manager while they walked.

"My first love: football," said David, his trainers squeaking on the polished hardwood flooring. "I'm a consultant for the local team. We moved into this building a couple of years ago." He fanned a hand about. "Can you believe this place used to house the large underground tanks of the station, now it's the best Fitness Centre in town. We've got professional athletes working-out and training alongside the public," he beamed proudly. "It's quite an interesting community."

"Wow," said the Young Manager, impressed. "You haven't got a soccer pitch down here, have you?"

Gary grinned. "Wait and see."

"So, the Pig Pen thing," said the Young Manager, changing tack, "I haven't really thought about how it could be used in sport, but I guess it can be applied to all manner of situations."

"Wherever there are problems and people, there is pig wrestling," said David. "The Pig Pen's definitely helped me get the very best results from the people I work with. Ah, here we are," he said, swinging open the door to his office.

After the glass-walled modernity of the gym, David's slightly old-fashioned leather and oak office decor took the Young Manager by surprise. The office was large and comfortable, with a wall of oak shelving that bore the weight of an extensive collection of medals, trophies, tributes, and sporting memorabilia. On one wall hung a huge whiteboard, with play diagrams scrawled in red marker pen. On another, a huge, curved TV screen played out the previous week's league game with the sound turned down. But what took the Young

Manager's breath away was the view from the window behind David's desk. It looked out over a large indoor football pitch: a massive rectangle of brilliant green, tucked away in a hidden cavern under the old turbine hall.

"This place is unbelievable!" exclaimed the Young Manager, striding over to the window, to marvel at the illuminated pitch below.

"Not a bad view given we're completely underground, right?" said David. "I told you this place was a Tardis. Drink?" He held out a bottle of mineral water, and the Young Manager took it gratefully. Then David led the way to a small round table with two Chesterfield armchairs, and invited the Young Manager to sit down.

"Okay, quick test," he said. "Can you recall the Pig Pen stages that you've covered so far? It's a good idea to reaffirm what you've learned in your mind, before moving on to the next three elements."

"I reckon I can," said the Young Manager, confidently. He visualised the Barista's original sketch. "Let's see," he began. "I walk up the hill to a pig pen, the size of a wrestling ring...I put my foot on the bottom rung of the fence and peer into the pen, where there's a big, muddy pig with a picture frame stuck around its neck. I look to my left and see a red bucket, with soapy water and a sponge...in the back left corner there's a tin feeding trough with the words *Made in Hanoi* embossed on it...um..."

"Go on," David said, encouragingly. "You're doing brilliantly."

"Oh! Of course," said the Young Manager. "I look at the top of the fence post on my right, and see a Crystal Ball. And that's everything we've covered, so far."

"Can you remember what comes next in the scene?"

"Yes, actually," said the Young Manager. "In the back right corner of the pen, there are gold nuggets embedded in the ground. The pig's trying to get to them, but he can't because he's held in place by two bright pink bungee cords. And at my feet there's a children's book. A book of spot the difference puzzles."

"Perfect," David said and smiled, giving a thumbs up, "Okay. Let's walk you through those last three elements of the scene. They all link together to provide a different way of thinking about problems, and a new approach to instigating change."

"Shoot!" said the Young Manager, as he tapped the screen of his tablet to life. "Let's get back to the Pen."

GOLD NUGGETS

"Let's take a look at those gold nuggets first," David began. "Kate will have told you all about the Crystal Ball and the Miracle Question, right?"

"Right," replied the Young Manager.

"And did you spend some time thinking about how you'd know if a miracle had occurred?" he asked.

"I still wish it was real," sighed the Young Manager.

David grinned and ran a hand through his shock of white hair. "What if I told you that the miracle you're waiting for had already happened?"

"It has?" the Young Manager replied, wracking his brain. "When?"

David took a swig of water from his bottle. "Let me explain," he said. "There are times when a problem is not a problem, or, as in your situation, as I understand it, times when a difficult person or team isn't difficult. So in those moments, however much of a problem you *think* you have, things will have been running perfectly smoothly at your office, albeit briefly— everyone getting on, work getting done. Unfortunately, we tend to focus on the difficult moments, so that these short interludes of success and peace are hidden away."

"Yeah," the Young Manager agreed. "I suppose there are flashes where everything's running smoothly. But it's hard to appreciate them in between the constant dramas. Besides, the smooth moments seem far fewer and further between, these days. Blink and you'll miss 'em."

"It can be hard," David acknowledged. "That's why you have to get proactively curious, and learn to positively notice these instances, these golden nuggets."

The Young Manager cast his mind back to earlier on. "This is what Gary was saying. Or something like it, anyway. We fail to spot those moments because we tend to generalise too quickly. And once we've put a frame around our problem, we don't pay any attention to any other perspective."

"Exactly," David nodded. "We delete those moments like they never happened and hold firm to our view that the *challenging situation* is a round-the-clock thing. But that's simply not true. The real gold lies in learning to spot those moments where your challenging team dynamic runs smoothly—or noting when that stubborn member of staff ditches their usual opposition. It might come down to any number of factors: a certain time of day, a certain environment, or the presence of a particular colleague. If you can pinpoint those instances, you can start to identify the right recipe for success. You just have to…"

Ask yourself, specifically, when and where does this problem not occur?

"It's also important to examine the times when your problematic situation is still there, but it isn't quite as disruptive as normal. Then you can start generating some insights."

"I don't think I've *ever* paid attention to the quiet moments in a storm, so to speak," said the Young Manager. "I let my thinking about certain problems become quite fixed."

"We all do it," said David. "Life seems less complicated when we allow ourselves to pigeon-hole things. But if you're struggling with a problem, that's not helpful. It's best to remain curious about the situations and behaviours you observe, to really explore where the limits and edges of the problems are. Exceptions to your problematic status quo might be fleeting, but they're always there."

The Young Manager cast his mind over the dysfunctional team dynamic that he had been trying so hard to improve. He thought about the times when the team's problems had been less of an issue—when conversations had been less tense, and ideas had flowed. And then it came to him…

"Come to think of it…" he muttered to himself.

"Go on," said David, smiling. "Share."

The Young Manager laughed. "Sorry. Only I think I might be onto something," he explained. "I'm just thinking about an instance with the two team leaders involved."

"Sounds interesting," said David, encouragingly.

"I've just realised that I'd been working on the assumption that meetings are always confrontational between their teams, because they get competitive in front of their opposite numbers, and that's down to their team leaders! Both of them encourage heated debate, and the whole thing usually blows up in everyone's faces. The thing is, now that I think about it, I can remember one meeting where things went very differently!"

"Tell me more," said David.

"It was a simple diary clash. Nothing more. One of the team leaders had a meeting they couldn't shift, and nobody had another window that worked, so instead of our usual full team roundtable, the two leaders and I nipped out for coffee at the end of the day, for a quick informal catch up. Well, in a more relaxed atmosphere, the usual drama just failed to materialise! It was a great meeting! We covered so much ground! I can't believe I've been ignoring that little moment of success." He paused and gritted his teeth. "The very next time we were all back in the boardroom, the fighting kicked off again. I suppose I got hooked up on *that* when I should have been thinking about what *worked* in the coffee shop."

"A perfect example of a *gold nugget*," said David. "When you've found one like that, it's really worth exploring it in more detail. Don't ignore it again!"

The Young Manager nodded vigorously. "I certainly won't," he said. "I'm going to try to keep all of these moments in mind."

"That's precisely what you need to do," David agreed. "It's about deliberately focussing your energy, attention and curiosity on the times that the problem *doesn't* happen. The times when the change that you're striving for, has already arrived." He sat back in his chair and beamed, broadly. "Then you can start to identify the *Pink Bungee Cords* that are pinning down your pig, and preventing the exception from becoming the norm."

PINK BUNGEE CORDS

"Let's think about the power of context," said David, expanding on his theme. "We like to think that people consciously choose how to act, but to a large extent context drives behaviour."

"You mean like the *context* of the office environment versus the coffee shop?" asked the Young Manager.

"In your case, yes," said David. "Context is a combination of people, politics, places, and power dynamics. You'd be surprised to learn exactly how much our own behaviour is affected by what occurs around us. Some social psychologists argue that *most* of our behaviour is driven by things like the environment, cultural norms, and societal structures."

"So we're mindless automata," said the Young Manager. "That's not a pretty picture."

David laughed. "Not quite," he explained, "but behaviours can be shaped and changed by altering the context in which they occur. That's the point. So as a manager, you need to consider how you would like your staff to behave and what context is most likely to encourage that behaviour. To do that, first you have to look at the context of your problem scenario, to find out exactly what's going wrong."

The Young Manager nodded his understanding as he added to his notes. "Go on," he said.

"We have a tendency to remove context from our assessments of problematic behaviour, in favour of scapegoating one of our colleagues," said David. "For instance, we attribute certain behaviours to negative character traits that we suppose they have."

"Aha!" said the Young manager in recognition. "That's the *Fundamental Attribution Error* that Gary told me about, isn't it?"

"That's right," said David. "When we judge others' actions, we all too often give too much causal weight to their supposed character, and not enough to the circumstances that shaped their actions. Then, even as we seek to understand the cause behind the problem, we will have already fallen into the traps of storytelling, labelling, and stereotyping. And round and round it goes," he added, turning circles with his wrist. "The *Pink Bungee Cords* are the contextual things that hold your problem in place. They pin the pig down in the mud."

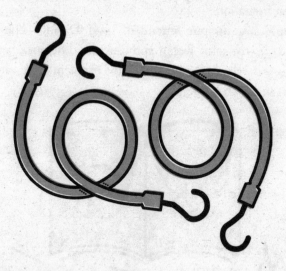

The Young Manager rubbed his chin thoughtfully and frowned at his notes. "So how do the Gold Nuggets and the Pink Bungee Cords come together?" he asked. "Do you twang the nuggets over the fence with the bungee cords, or what?"

David laughed aloud at the idea. "I like it"—he guffawed—"sounds sort of sporty, you know, which is absolutely my thing…but no…"

SPOT THE DIFFERENCE

"Tell me what followed the bungee cords in the pig-pen mnemonic again," David continued.

"It was the *Spot the Difference* book," said the Young Manager, without hesitation.

"Spot on, no pun intended," said David. "The book reminds us the trick lies in spotting the difference between two contexts, the context in which the problem occurs and the context in which it doesn't."

"And it's really that simple?" asked the Young Manager.

"Simple, yes. That doesn't necessarily mean it's easy," said David, echoing Kate's words. "You've got to take care not to engage in dirty thinking—no storytelling or second guessing the underlying cause of your problems. It comes down to this: you have to…"

Get curious about the times the problem reliably occurs, and explore the context around it.

"Try to identify who is and isn't present when the trouble starts," David continued. "Think about the time and location of events. Consider what's going on whilst the problem occurs, what might be feeding into the problem that you've identified, and acknowledge which set of rules are being played to. Keep a list, is my advice. That way you won't leave anything out."

"So how many factors do I need to bear in mind when I'm doing this?" asked the Young Manager.

"That's a bit like asking how many pockets you need to look in before you find your keys," said David. "It differs from one situation to the next, depending on how quickly you find the specific context that's triggering your problem. But in every case, you need to get to the point where you could wilfully engineer a context that you know with absolute certainty would trigger the problem you're trying to tackle."

"Why would I want to rattle the tiger's cage like that?" asked the Young Manager.

"You wouldn't," said David. "The point isn't to cause trouble. It's to learn exactly *how* the problem pattern is maintained, to the point where you could reliably recreate it on demand."

"You know, I should bring my sister in on this method," said the Young Manager, light-heartedly. "You should see her kids when they want ice cream."

David chuckled and went on. "Understanding how to engineer a problem from scratch, allows you to pinpoint the precise context in which it occurs. Once you've done that…"

Follow the same process for times when the problem *doesn't* occur, and spot the difference between the two contexts.

"Ah, so that's where the book comes in," said the Young Manager as the penny dropped.

"Right," David replied. "And once you've spotted the key differences, it's simply a matter of consistently shaping the *context* so that it more mirrors the times when the problem doesn't occur."

"That all makes sense in theory," said the Young Manager, "but can you give me an example, so I get my head around how it might work in practice?"

"No problem," said David, warmly. "Let's see…okay. There's this player I've been helping the local club with, whose form has been up and down, all over the place."

The Young Manager sat forward, resting his elbows on his knees, eager to hear what David had to say.

"He's a striker," the older man went on, "had a fantastic season last year. Phenomenal! But this year, well…" He shook his head. "At away games he was fine. Moved well. Really took the ball to the opposition. Had a massive impact on the mind-set of the whole team. But whenever we played at home," he continued, "he underperformed badly! He was half the player he could be whenever he was in front of a home crowd. I mean, you'd think the home fans would be a boost if anything, right" David sighed heavily. "I had theories being offered left, right, and centre. Some people reckoned it was down to the pressure on him, the weight of expectation that a home fixture brought. Others thought that the home fans had been getting on his back too much before he'd had a chance to get back on track, and throwing him off even more. I didn't buy those stories. You see, when you looked at the hard facts, there were times he *had* performed well at home. They just weren't coming along often enough."

"So you looked at the context?" asked the Young Manager intrigued.

"I got curious," David replied with a smile. "I looked at the times when he'd performed well and the times when he hadn't. Obviously there were lots of differences of context between playing at home and playing away, so it wasn't until I looked at the rare moments when he'd played well at home that the truth dawned on me."

"So what was it that was making the difference?"

"Well, to cut a long story short, it turned out that on the times when he'd played well in front of the home crowd, he'd actually stayed away."

"Come again?" said the Young Manager, confused.

"He'd stayed away from home…*his* home. For the games he'd played well in, the team schedule meant he'd stayed at the club's official hotel the night before the game, rather than heading home as normal," David explained. "He had twin babies at home, you see. He didn't want to admit it to his wife, but he was losing way too much sleep. Once we identified that as the key factor, we knew exactly how to resolve the problem. And I'm happy to say, his wife was very reasonable about the situation too, when I explained what was going on. He's their leading scorer again this season. He spends nights before the home games in the hotel, and his Mrs. gets a monthly visit to a treatment spa with the club's sincere gratitude."

"And all it took was one small change," said the Young Manager, impressed.

"A little thing, yes. But one that I wouldn't have spotted without the pig pen," said David, tapping his temple with a finger. "So, do you see how finding that one key difference could help you make progress with your own staff problems?"

"Absolutely," the Young Manager replied at once. He scrolled through his notes to recap. "Let me run through this," he said. "That's *my* system for getting things clear in my head…

SUMMARY

- Ask yourself *where* and *when* a problem occurs, as well as *where* and *when* it does *not*.

- Get curious about the times when the problem can be relied upon to raise itself, and explore the context of those occasions.

- Do the same for the times when the problem does *not* occur and try to spot the difference between the occurrences and nonoccurrences.

"You've got it," David stated. "If you can think about problems in this way, you'll open up all sorts of new routes to positive change. You'll be able to unlock the full potential of all sorts of people on your team."

"Thank you," said the Young Manager, as they rose to their feet together. "This has definitely changed the way I think about problems."

"And how you'll approach them in the future, I hope," said David.

"You bet," said the Young Manager, shaking hand, firmly.

"That's good to hear," said David. "I'm sure I'll see you around the place, probably at Courtyard Coffee. And feel free to come in and use the machines, if you fancy a workout. I'll give you some training tips if you like, but I have to warn you, I don't mess about," he winked.

The Young Manager glanced at his watch, time was ticking on, but he was on a path now, and he was determined to see it through. "Thanks and this has all been great," he offered, gently, "but do you mind me asking how many more people there are for me to meet today?"

"Don't worry." David smiled. "You're almost done." He gave the Young Manager a hearty slap on the back. "You've just got Andrea to go. She'll walk you through the final two elements of the pig-pen scene, then you'll have the whole process. What you do with it…well…*the ball's in your court* as we say in sporting circles."

The Young Manager left the basement gym, his head churning with the things he had learnt so far. As he entered the elevator that would take him to the roof garden, he was more confident than he had been for a long while that he could turn around his company's people problem.

As the Young Manager ran through the conversations that he'd be having with his team on his return, he could feel his energy levels rising. For the first time ever, the problems he was tackling actually brought a smile to his face. The miracle he'd been waiting for just might have already happened!

SWITCHING

The Young Manager walked through a set of glass doors onto a roof garden bathed in sunlight. David had pointed him up there for his final meeting. He'd never been up to the roof before, though all of the Collective's tenants had access to it. He'd never found the time. Now he wished that he had. He stopped for a moment to breathe in the scene. It was late June so the garden was full of colour, contrasting against the city's skyline of brick, steel, and glass buildings of every shape and size. The rustling of the roof garden's plants in the gentle breeze didn't quite drown out the noise of the traffic below, but as the Young Manager picked his way along a path between flower beds, it was easy to forget that he was in the heart of the city.

"Hello," said a voice from behind a potted olive tree near the building's edge, "over here."

Andrea Strenson leaned out from the bench she was sitting on, clearing the slender trunk of the olive tree, and waved, casually. She was an elegant woman in her sixties, wearing well-coordinated purple outfit that blended perfectly with the rooftop flora.

"Hi!" the Young Manager called out, strolling over to join her on the bench, "You must be Andrea. It's amazing up here, isn't it?"

Andrea nodded. "It's my very favourite spot in the city, I think." She smiled, spreading her arms as if to embrace the view. "Did you know that every plant up here is edible, medicinal, or otherwise useful?"

"I did not," admitted the Young Manager. "To be perfectly honest, this is the first time I've been up here."

Andrea looked positively shocked.

"What a waste!" she exclaimed. "My dear boy, life can all too easily become all consuming and difficult. You simply must find the time to catch your breath and think...to get perspective. These are often the moments when we gain the most powerful insights."

Feeling somewhat chastened, the Young Manager could do no more than nod sheepishly. Andrea was right, of course. Why *hadn't* he been up here? Why had he never thought to bring his staff up here for meetings, for that matter? What a glorious space to use on a sunny day! It was hard to imagine tensions running high in this urban oasis.

"Now then, to business," said Andrea briskly, interrupting his train of thought. "I'm sure you've had quite enough of all this talk today. Are you ready to learn about the last two elements of the Pig Pen? That's the *Green Recycling Bin* and the *Yellow Warning Sign*, if you remember the mnemonic."

"Yes, I remember," said the Young Manager, "and yes, absolutely yes! I'm good to go!"

GREEN RECYCLING BIN

"I'll start with a warning," said Andrea, ominously. "Anything done to excess—anything *overdone*—will eventually become toxic." She swivelled on the bench so that they were face to face. "The problems we find ourselves wrestling with are often born out of previously successful strategies that have been *overdone* and as such, outlived their usefulness."

"Can you elaborate?" asked the Young Manager.

"Of course," Andrea replied. She leaned back against the bench again and stared around the roof garden. "Everyone has their own preferred ways of going about things, don't they?" she began. "Maybe because of their upbringing, their education, their character, or their expertise…whatever it is that informs those methods, they will have helped to achieve positive results in the past, so they naturally became the default way of working or behaving." She held up a finger to indicate a warning. "A problem occurs when those default approaches *fail*, because the truth is, most people tend to just carry on regardless, engaging in more of the same."

"Like they just default to type," offered the Young Manager.

"Exactly," said Andrea, "exactly that." She rummaged in a large leather handbag at her feet and fished out a packet of custard creams. "Help yourself," she said, tearing open the packet and placing it on the bench between them. "In my experience," she said, with a wry smile, "young men are often peckish."

"Thanks," said the Young Manager, popping a biscuit straight in his mouth. It was probably approaching lunchtime by now, he supposed. He hadn't had time to think about his stomach, but he *was* growing hungry.

"An example," said Andrea, switching straight back to her theme. "Imagine that someone has enjoyed success in the past by being strong willed and consistently sure of their course of action, even in the face of doubters. That sort of attitude can easily grow out of a period in a tough management role. So, it becomes their default way of operating." She paused and raised her eyebrows. "Then, one day, they find themselves in a situation they haven't faced before, one where their tried-and-tested bullish methods do not work. And the more they try, the more they fail. They just keep hammering away, assuming that everyone and everything else is *wrong*. That the world has gone mad." Andrea rolled her eyes. "That's when *other* people start labelling *them*. They're *stubborn*. They're *pig headed*. But it's really not their fault," she explained. "They're just stuck in the mud."

"Is this where the Green Recycling Bin comes in?" asked the Young Manager, helping himself to another biscuit.

"It is indeed," said Andrea tapping the tip of her nose. "When we find ourselves stuck with a problem, we often talk about the people or teams involved in terms of what we perceive to be their negative traits. They're *disengaged, unmotivated,* or *difficult.* Sound familiar?"

The Young Manager nodded, "Unfortunately, it does, yes."

Andrea laughed, softly. "We've found that it's more effective to think of each of these traits as overdone strengths," she said. "Then we can concentrate on redirecting the efforts of a team or a team member, to reapply their talents and energies more positively."

"Hmm," the Young Manager said as he mused. "I'm not convinced all traits are strengths."

"Personality traits are never purely good or bad," said Andrea. "It's not as cut and dried as that. I believe it was Aristotle who said that any virtue that is under- or overdone can become a vice. Being ambitious, for example, is often looked upon favourably in corporate circles. However, when it's overdone, it can be interpreted as greed, or the unmitigated drive for power. Know that. Own it. Use it. Our vices, might just be overegged virtues. Even moaning can have its merits. You see…"

By viewing problems as the result of overdone strengths, creating change becomes less about fixing deficits, and more about redirecting energy.

"Again, you have to recognise the power of your language." She continued, "Once we label the behaviour as being negative, it's very difficult to see it's positive potential. Take David's footballers, for example. At his best, a player's fans might describe him as *instinctive* and *passionate*. But as soon as his form dips, those same people will no longer see those traits as positive attributes. They'll use words like *impulsive* and *hot headed* to describe the very same attributes that they previously celebrated. He's the same person doing the same thing, but when you're not getting the results you want, you're more likely to choose, subconsciously of course, to see him in a negative light."

"Yes, I see what you mean," said the Young Manager, nodding. "So, in Pig Pen language, I guess you're saying that we need to look past the labelling and framing of our problems, clean our thinking and identify the strengths beneath."

"You *have* been listening." Andrea smiled. "Quite so. Clean the problem and explore how supposed negatives could actually be turned into positive, constructive attributes."

"That's certainly a more productive way to view people," the Young Manager acknowledged. "I like it."

"Milton Erickson, a thinker I very much admire, said this," Andrea said,

> '*Every person's map of the world is as unique as their thumbprint. There are no two people alike. No two people who understand the same sentence the same way. So in dealing with people, try not to fit them to your concept of what they should be.*'

"I like to commit quotes to memory," she added. "Whenever you work with people, if you're curious and open minded, you'll come to learn far more about them than their job title alone might reveal. And as you do so, you may well stumble across the very *best* of their character, talents, and passions. All of that information is priceless when you're trying to find ways to get the best out of people at work. And of course, in the Pig Pen, it links to the idea of gold nuggets—finding exceptions to your problematic situations."

They watched for a moment as a scruffy sparrow landed on one of the raised flower beds, pecked a bug from among the leaves, and flew off, chirruping triumphantly.

"Marvellous, isn't it?" Andrea said, enthusiastically. "You don't get *that* in the boardroom!" She paused and brushed a fallen leaf from her lap. "Often, you're better off finding the resources that are already there, the ones that have been dismissed or have so far gone un-noticed. Such resources are inherent in everyone, in every situation, latent, ready to be used and applied. Using these is often much more effective than trying to teach someone a new way of behaving or create something completely from scratch. It's about recycling and reusing, just like the edible or medicinal qualities of these plants all around us—all of them containing hidden powers, if we only seek to notice." She turned and patted the Young Manager on the arm. "My dear boy," she said. "Your job as a leader is to lay the groundwork for your staff's success. You have to bring out their brightest colours and let them shine…"

Help people apply the skills inherent in their talents, passions, and problems, and you'll find it much easier to create the change that you need.

"That sounds like common sense," said the Young Manager.

"I'm glad you think so," said Andrea. "Because that tells me that you're ready for the final piece of the picture."

YELLOW WARNING SIGN

"Let's quickly go over a few reminders for when you find yourself pig wrestling," said Andrea. "Firstly…"

Pigs aren't pets: Beware of taking problems home with you. Don't grow accustomed to their presence by your side.

"You don't strike me as the sort," Andrea explained, "but there are some managers who quite plainly enjoy having something to complain about. They secretly like those problems that stick with them, through good times and bad, like an annoying old friend. Well that nonsense is no good for anyone, least of all the people involved in the problem. So, you've got to take the time to clean your thinking about the problems you are tackling. Not just five minutes here or there, or in the early hours of the morning, devoting proper time to this is paramount otherwise you will remain stuck in inertia."

The Young Manager nodded as he scribbled his customary notes on his tablet device, and helped himself to a third custard cream.

"Secondly" said Andrea, somewhat melodramatically…

Beware imaginary pigs. All too often, the problems we should be tackling lie within ourselves.

"How do you mean?" asked the Young Manager.

"What I've said applies in two ways," Andrea explained. "Leaders can cause themselves immense distress by playing out all sorts of imaginary, hypothetical situations in their minds. Planning for future problems, so to speak. Then they move about the workplace, relating to colleagues and situations as if their pessimistic visions had already come to pass." She rubbed her fingers together as if they were dirty. "It's a contamination.

That's why it's vital to clean one's thinking and hold firmly to the facts."

"And the other way?" the Young Manager enquired.

"Sometimes the problems with which we wrestle are driven by an unrealistic view of the world," said Andrea. "We tell ourselves that teammates should always get along, that people should be totally engaged at work at all times, and that we should always be happy. None of those things are possible or true, but *believing* that they should be still leads us back into the mud of the pig pen, time and time again. That's when you find yourself trying to tackle an unsolvable problem, based on a false reality. An imaginary pig!" She threw her hands up in despair. "And ultimately, it's *your* twisted view of reality that's the *real* pig in the room."

The Young Manager sighed wearily and flopped back on the bench. "I have wondered whether *I'm* the problem from time to time," he admitted.

"Of course you have," said Andrea, her bright eyes boring into him, "and of course you *are*. That's really what you've been learning with all of us, isn't it? My dear boy, don't you see, this is *all* about you…"

Problem cleaning means untangling our own thinking so that we can find a more effective strategy to create the change that we need.

The Young Manager felt like he'd been hit with a thunderbolt. Of *course* it was about him. Only *he* was the Captain of his own ship, and now at last he had the map he needed to steer it off the rocks and into calmer waters. He'd bring out the very best in his staff, and himself while he was at it.

"Thank you, Andrea," he said quietly. "This has been quite the slap in the face, but I needed it."

"Short sharp shock. Works wonders, dear. Biscuit?" she asked, holding out the half empty pack.

The Young Manager chuckled. "I'd better not," he said. "I've blown my sugar allowance for the week already." He paused to skim over his notes. "Do you mind if I just go through this once before I leave?"

Andrea nodded for him to go on.

SUMMARY

- Try to see problems as the result of overdone strengths, instead of faults. Think less about fixing deficits and more about redirecting energies.
- Help people to apply the skills that reflect their core talents and passions, and you'll find it much easier to create the change you need.
- Pigs aren't pets. Don't take your problems home with you, and don't grow accustomed to having them by your side.
- Beware imaginary pigs. And make sure the problem isn't *you*!
- Problem cleaning untangles our thinking to unlock new and successful strategies.

"That's a wonderful summary," said Andrea supportively. "You've clearly taken on board everything you've heard." She smiled warmly at the Young Manager and patted his arm. "And now I think it's time for you to go back to where your little adventure started. Meet the boss again."

"The boss?" said the Young Manager. "The Barista, you mean? In the lobby."

Andrea laughed. "If that's what you say, dear," she said, mysteriously.

CLOSING

"My word! The pig wrestler returns!" boomed the old barista from his counter as the Young Manager approached. "I wondered when you'd show up." He jiggled his magnificent bushy eyebrows. "You, if I may be so bold, look like a man who could do with a good coffee."

"You're right about that," said the Young Manager, smacking his lips at the thought of one of the Barista's delicious brews.

The Barista got to work on a flat white, while the Young Manager folded his arms on the kiosk counter and watched patiently. He felt happy and relaxed, even as his mind buzzed with all the new information from Andrea, and perhaps the sugar rush from her Custard Creams.

"I should thank you again, for all the introductions," he said to the Barista's back. "It's been a fascinating tour."

"There's really no need," said the Barista, over his shoulder. "I'm very happy to help. I know the look of a man who's stuck in the pig pen and needs a way out. So, how did you find it all?"

"Extremely constructive and enlightening," said the Young Manager, "especially when it comes to the team dynamic problem that's been keeping me up at night."

"Go on," the Barista encouraged him. "Talk me through it."

"I think I'd rather like to, actually," said the Young Manager. He gathered his thoughts and began. "First, the foot on the fence checks made me realise the specific part of the issue between the teams that is *my* pig to wrestle, and it also underlined that I *do* need to tackle it right away. It's been going on for way too long, and I need to own it," he sighed. "The conflict between my teams is impacting some of our key business objectives and our performance is suffering, so there's no shelving this issue for later."

"Good start," said the Barista. "And what did you take from Gary, with his problem-cleaning tools?"

"That I needed to challenge the frame that was around the pig's neck. I'd framed my problem as a team dynamics issue. After my chat with Gary, I began to see that I could, in fact, frame the situation in any number of different ways."

"Such as?" asked the Barista, steaming milk as the espresso dripped through his machine.

"Well, I might just as easily have viewed it as a leadership problem, or a communication breakdown, or a cultural clash, or even a procedural issue," the Young Manager explained. "That part of the mnemonic helped me to realise that the frame I *had* was not a helpful one, and gave me the freedom to challenge it."

The Barista turned towards the counter, nodding. "Realising that the frame can change is often the first step in resolving a longstanding problem, as I'm sure Gary told you."

"He did indeed," said the Young Manager. "Gary's red bucket and sponge also helped me to see that I was using unhelpful language and labels to describe the problem…that I needed to scrub those away and clean up my thinking."

"Good man," boomed the Barista. "Don't think for a moment that I didn't spot the dirty thinking when we first met, in your initial assessment of your problems," he added, smiling.

"I know, I know," said the Young Manager, holding up his hands in mock surrender. "I also realised that I'd been treating my problem as though it was *always* happening, which it really isn't. Gary helped me to redescribe the situation. Kate's tin feeding trough was a help too. I honestly thought I'd tried everything. But, of course, I was simply trying variations of the same solution over and over again and expecting different results. Just like the people of Hanoi, my attempted solutions were actually making the problem worse, not better!"

"I bet that left you wondering where you were headed," chuckled the Barista. "What did you make of the miracle question?"

"Ah yes, the magical crystal ball," said the Young Manager, remembering Kate's rather sad photocopied stand-in. "When I thought about how I would know when my problem had been solved, I realised that the problem wasn't really about the two teams working together as a whole at all."

"That sounds like a seismic shift frame-wise," said the Barista. "What *was* the problem, then?"

"Well, once I'd examined my *nice-to-haves* and my *need-to-haves*, I quickly became aware that I had plenty of the former clouding my thinking. It would be *nice* if the teams got on really well. It would be *nice* if the managers could be pleasant to one another in our Monday morning briefings. It would be *nice* if they were friends…" The Young Manager paused. "But when you get down to brass tacks, what I *need* is much simpler. What I *need* is for the two team leaders to agree where we are with the project, and keep me regularly updated on their progress."

The Barista handed the Young Manager a steaming mug of coffee with an elaborate leaf design perfectly poured into the milk. "This one's on me," he said and smiled. "It feels as though your muddy pig of a problem might be rather more pink and clean than it was before."

The Young Manager nodded. "Definitely. And thanks," he said, raising his coffee. "But it was when I met David to learn about the golden nuggets that I had my first major insight. When I turned my mind to the times when my problem *wasn't* a problem, that's when I found a gold nugget hiding in plain sight!"

"I do love a eureka moment," beamed the Barista.

"The main issue, I now realise, is a clash between my two team leaders, driven by a specific context." The Young Manager explained, "When I set about spotting the differences between the times when the problem occurred and the times when things had gone well, that factor became obvious. I realised that the two managers are driving a tendency towards excessive competition between their teams. That's what makes the meetings so fraught. Whereas when I meet with the managers alone, in an informal setting, they get on much better, and are far more productive. So my frame shifted completely, from a 'team dynamics' problem, to something more like a 'meeting scheduling' problem."

"Now that *is* a useful insight," said the Barista. "And to think, you'd have missed it if you hadn't been looking. Then it was Andrea, wasn't it? What did you make of her?"

"She was great," the Young Manager exclaimed. "When Andrea spoke to me about the green recycling bin, and the idea that weaknesses are often *overdone* strengths, I realised that the two managers in question are actually very similar. Both are highly competitive, somewhat headstrong, and very direct in their approach. But these strengths, overdone, have come to be viewed negatively by both teams, fuelling gossip, storytelling, and labelling, which has been leading to further antagonism."

"So," asked the Barista, "do you have a way forward now?"

"You know what?" said the Young Manager. "I think I do." He sipped his coffee. "It came to me as I worked through the mnemonic with everyone this morning. I'm going to scrap the individual updates in our Monday morning team meetings, and arrange to meet the two managers informally the Friday before. Then on Mondays, I'll ask them to present a joint update to both teams. I think I can turn that competitive trait that's been overdone lately into a strength and get them collaborating for the best result. And with the credit shared equally at team meetings, things should be a lot calmer all round."

"That sounds like an excellent plan," said the Barista, "and a fine example of how all the elements of the pig pen can work together." He raised an eyebrow and leaned across the counter. "But there's one more thing, isn't there?"

"There is?" said the Young Manager, scratching his head.

"The Yellow Warning Sign, my boy," boomed the Barista. "No more wrestling with your problems at three in the morning!"

The Young Manager laughed. "I certainly hope not," he said.

"Indulge my curiosity for a moment," said the Barista. "What would you say was the key message for you *personally* speaking?"

The Young Manager thought for a moment. There had been so many lessons; so many elements of the pig-pen mnemonic that had resonated with him. How could he pick just one?

"I think," he began, after careful consideration, "for me, it's all about making sure that before I attempt to solve any problem, I should take the time to find the right problem to tackle. I can't begin to tell you how much money and effort has been misdirected trying to fix the wrong problems!"

The Barista nodded. "I can well imagine. Resources are too valuable to be wasted." The Barista continued, "The Pig Pen cuts to the chase." He karate chopped the air, playfully, with one huge hand. "It helps to unlock the hidden value in your organisation. It's a bona fide secret power, enabling leaders nurture their people in far more intelligent and productive ways." He smiled, enigmatically. "The results speak for themselves."

"And I for one can't wait to try it out," said the Young Manager.

"And I look forward to hearing about the results," said the Barista, rubbing his hands together eagerly. "And do remember, that the framework isn't just about people problems. It works with any kind of longstanding problem."

"Really?" the Young Manager asked.

The Barista smiled and nodded. "Oh yes, by using this framework I've known people to be able to rethink processes, adapt procedures, design training programmes, and even shape their leadership teams."

"I see what you mean," replied the Young Manager, nodding his head.

"They're just problems, after all," said the Barista. "And they will all involve someone wrestling with a situation, making assumptions, and limiting their thinking. The Pig Pen is just as useful in situations like these."

"What about you, then?" asked the Young Manager, his own curiosity piqued. "What about the whole Pig Pen thing speaks to you?"

The Barista looked surprised to be asked the question. Then his face broke into a warm smile.

"Well," he shrugged, "I guess I'd have to say that in business, just as in life…"

We simply cannot afford to be spending time and money, applying misguided strategies to poorly conceived and ill-defined problems.

"Well, it's worked for your coffee stall," said the Young Manager. "I've never known a more popular offering in its field."

The Barista chuckled. "Thank you, young man. I appreciate the compliment. Now, just one last thing before we both get back to work," said the Barista. "I don't suppose you had a moment to consider my nightmare neighbour problem, did you?"

"Actually, yes!" said the Young Manager. "It came to mind after I'd met with Kate, the solution seems pretty obvious, in retrospect."

"Do tell!" The Barista beamed.

"Well," the Young Manager explained, "I was thinking about your problem, and about the Crystal Ball, and it occurred to me that it would be *nice* if your neighbour was motivated to shut the gates. And it would be *nice* if he was as concerned about your family's safety as you are. I hope you don't take this the wrong way, but your early solutions were all ways to encourage those *nice* outcomes, instead of looking at your *needs*."

"No offence taken," said the Barista, "good observation."

"What you actually *needed*," the Young Manager continued, "was for the gates to stay shut. In essence, you didn't have a neighbour problem, you had a gate shutting problem."

"Aha!" the leader said with a smile. "Well now, that would open all manner of fresh possibilities, wouldn't it?"

"That's what I thought," the Young Manager replied. "Automatic gates would do the trick. Maybe even something as simple as a spring!"

"I like your thinking," said the Barista. "And so much easier to tackle than a difficult neighbour."

"Was that was how you solved it in the end, then?" the Young Manager asked.

"Nope," said the Barista, bluntly.

"Eh?" said, the Young Manager, crestfallen.

"Do you recall the Foot on the Fence checks?" asked the Barista. "Because, as it happens, they could have helped to resolve my own dilemma in its very early stages."

"I'm not sure I understand," said the Young Manager. "How would they have altered your course? It was clear how it was a problem for you, and you needed to tackle it straight away, before someone went under a lorry! And you'd seen the situation in the flesh, so you were well informed, weren't you?"

The Barista chuckled. "Right on all counts, except for the last piece. I hadn't really seen the whites of the pig's eyes. In fact, my perspective on reality was less reliable than I assumed," he said, mysteriously. "You see, the day after the sign had been taken down—the reminder I'd put up about closing our shared gate—I had to go into the office a little earlier than usual to prepare for an important meeting. So, almost at the crack of dawn, I found myself standing once more with my family's puppy, in the front garden of our house. And I saw something I hadn't seen before. I saw our neighbour leaving for work!"

"You caught him in the act, you mean?" asked the Young Manager.

"I rather thought I might," said the Barista. "I watched him roll down the driveway to our shared gates. He got out of his car and opened them. Then he climbed back in and drove slowly drove through. I was ready to leap out at that point, let me tell you, and confront him with his crimes. Then he stopped…got out of his car again…closed the gates behind himself like a dutiful neighbour, and drove off to work. To be frank I was rather annoyed. I knew he was the problem, and I'd wanted some concrete proof!"

"I don't get it," said the Young Manager.

"I haven't finished," said the Barista and winked. "A few moments after my neighbour had left, shutting the gates behind him, a huge procession of highway construction trucks thundered past in convoy. The work had been going on nearby for months, but I'd never been up to see their early-morning rush hour before, and our double glazing had kept me ignorant of noise from the road. There must have been a thousand tonnes of heavy duty vehicles thundering past our front gates…and as they did, shaking the very ground beneath my feet, the latch on those old gates rattled open, and the gates swung wide open, all on their own."

"You're kidding!" exclaimed the Young Manager.

"I'm not," the Barista replied. "The vibrations from the convoy of trucks must have dislodged the latch that kept the gates shut." He grimaced. "Well, I immediately realised what a pig I had been, and I use the word advisedly," he winked. "That solved the mystery of why the gates remained shut at weekends, too. The building site only operated from Monday to Friday."

"So your neighbour had stuck to his word the whole time?" the Young Manager asked.

"From day one," said the Barista. "Which is why he'd seemed so defiant when I challenged him, and so taken aback by my emotional outburst."

"Ouch"—the Young Manager winced—"awkward. But it still doesn't excuse his taking down the sign that you put up, does it?"

"You're right; it probably wouldn't," the Barista agreed. "But it turns out that the poor chap didn't do that either. My sign had actually blown off the gate by the wind. I found it later that week, lodged in lower branches of a nearby tree."

"Your neighbour never was the problem at all, then," the Young Manager said slowly. "You got the wrong pig, and then your own confirmation bias held it in place. Right?"

"Exactly right," replied the Barista. "If only I had taken the time to examine the situation fully, to stay curious and avoid labelling—if only I'd looked into the differences between the times when the problem occurred and those when it didn't—I might have nipped it in the bud much sooner. But that experience taught me an important lesson, it showed me that…"

When you're quick to judge, you will often find yourself surrounded by pigs.

"I want to keep my life as pig-free as possible," said the Young Manager. "I've got a lot of thinking to do, but at least I know that I've got the tools to clean my problems now. I can see a better way forward. To be honest, I can't *wait* to get started!"

"That's what we like to hear." The Barista smiled. He glanced over the Young Manager's shoulder. People were appearing from offices and trickling towards him like slow-moving lava. It was almost lunch time. "I knew you'd take to the pig pen like a duck to water, if I can mix my farmyard metaphors for a moment." The Barista chuckled. "Of course, now comes the hard part. You have the wisdom, it's what you do with it that counts." He paused for a moment to study the Young Manager; his face was serious, but his eyes sparkled with energy and determination. "Live it, or leave it," said the old barista. "The choice is yours."

"Oh, I'm going to live it," said the Young Manager, firmly. "You just watch me go!"

RETURNING

The weeks passed quickly after the Young Manager's introduction to the pig pen, and while he saw the Barista often enough, there was never quite time to talk. Either he was too busy or the Barista was. But he did take Kate up on her offer of coffee, and he submitted to David's punishing training regime at the basement gym.

Office life was good. The new way of thinking was working, and morale was soaring. They were holding an impromptu office party on the roof garden later that very evening, to celebrate a particularly big deal as well as to make the most of the view while the warm evenings lasted. The Young Manager had so much to thank the Barista for, and he was determined to invite him along to that evening's event as his guest of honour. But when he approached the Courtyard Coffee Shack, he was surprised to see a smiley twentysomething woman standing behind the counter instead.

"Hi," said the Young Manager, "I was looking for the usual guy."

The woman's smile widened. "He's away for a bit, seeing to his other ventures," she explained.

"Other ventures?" asked the Young Manager, surprised. "So, does he own more than one coffee stand?"

The woman burst out laughing. "You don't know, do you?"

"Know what?" asked the Young Manager, completely confused.

"Um, that he *owns* the building?" said the woman. "Not just this one, either."

She waved a hand about airily, and a cluster of silver bangles jangled loudly on her wrist. "There's other stuff too, but you kind of lose count after a while."

"I…I didn't realise!" stuttered the Young Manager. "I'd just assumed he had this stand!" he blurted out, still in shock. "My God!"

"He converted this whole place. Not bad for the son of a pig farmer is it?" the woman at the counter added with a smile. "Over the years he's been involved in all sorts of things, but whatever he's done, he's always believed in the power of bringing people together, in supporting one another to create change. That's why it's called the Collective. I also think he kind of liked the idea of an old power station too. Generating a new energy…a new way of thinking…empowering people."

The Young Manager didn't know what to say or do. He felt like such an idiot.

He had been looking at the Barista through the wrong frame the whole time. He'd labelled him as just an old barista, despite the fact that this incredible man had fired him up with the best advice he'd ever been given. He'd wasted so much time—if only he'd opened his eyes sooner and recognised what he really needed. While the Young Manager had busied himself wrestling pigs, too caught up to even get his own morning coffee, he'd missed the golden nugget that had been waiting in plain sight all along.

"I can see by your face that this is all a bit of a shock," said the woman, clearly amused. She reached out to shake his hand. "I'm his granddaughter. I look after this place when he's elsewhere. He keeps the stand as a sort of informal advice booth for anyone who needs it. Technically, he's retired. You might want to tell him that next time you see him, because he doesn't seem to listen to me!"

"I came down to tell him about some work thing he helped me with actually," said the Young Manager, still shaken by this new discovery.

"The Pig Pen, right?" asked the young woman. "Great stuff. It's all about relationships really, isn't it? Your relationship with yourself and your thoughts, your relationships with others and their behaviour. It kind of transforms how you view the world around you. It certainly worked wonders on my boyfriend problem. Well, *ex*-boyfriend. Like I say, it worked wonders," she grinned.

The Young Manager grinned back. "Mine was more of a work thing," he said.

"Anyway, don't worry. He'll be back here at some point soon," said the Barista's granddaughter. "He comes and goes. I think he enjoys the *mysterious-business-guru* vibe. I'll tell him you were looking for him. He'll want to catch up. He *always* does. He's always keen to know when someone has gotten out of the pig pen and created the change they need." She grinned again. "Now, how about a coffee? According to my grandad, I make the second-best brew in the city."

[The End]

AFTERWORD

As you might have guessed, we're both big fans of fables. We love their accessibility and how they take the reader on a journey, conveying important and complex messages relatively indirectly. But as with any fable, the true power of this book lies in helping you, and those who you care for, in acting more effectively from this point onwards.

We wrote this book with the aim of helping you clean your thinking when you find yourself 'stuck', and helping you avoid getting 'stuck' in the first place. Our hope is for you to be able to find new ways to view challenging situations, to find new avenues to explore, and find ways to create the change that you need.

We've met some people who are able to read this short fable and immediately apply the principles contained within it. Others, learn the mnemonic and the key principles contained within the book, but need more conscious effort to apply it to their own situation.

Whether you're struggling with a situation in your professional or personal life, we'd suggest taking the time to reflect on the story and the lessons contained within it. Despite its brevity, the story covers some very significant concepts that once grasped can have a profound impact on the quality of your life.

Many people benefit from reading the story more than once. After all, reading and rereading is the only way to make anything we read a part of us. A second read through can really aid in grasping the full meaning of the lessons and their application.

On subsequent readings, you might benefit from imagining a scenario where you are currently struggling to create the change that you need. In doing so, try applying the principles to this situation, translating it to fit your own world.

Reflecting in this way can begin the process of problem cleaning, identifying new avenues to explore and new strategies to employ. To aid with this reflection, in the pages that follow, we've also included a simple visual overview of the stages of Problem Cleaning.

But there's another way to really bring the lessons contained in this fable to life…share them!

Tell others about the pig pen, ask them the questions, pass on the story.

Spot the pigs that you and others have been wrestling with, begin discussing the principles with colleagues, explore what you can immediately apply in your world.

Just like the Barista and the Collective, we've learnt that once this language and way of thinking is adopted by groups, individuals proactively begin supporting one another in cleaning their thinking. It seems to work best when everyone in a team or company knows both the story and the pig pen mnemonic. As the language spreads deeper into teams and organisations, it seems to become especially effective.

So the next time you're in a meeting and someone declares that we have a 'communication', 'cultural' or 'team dynamics' problem, consider using the crystal ball and ask them, *"How would we know that this problem was solved?"*

Should you find yourself claiming that you have tried 'everything' to solve a problem, be prepared to explore what's in the feeding trough and ask, *"Exactly what have we tried?"*, *"What do these solutions have in common?"* and *"What made the problem better or worse?"* Maybe even check if the previous solutions were simply putting lipstick on the pig!

Should you hear someone state that a problem has 'always' been around, encourage them to search for the golden nuggets, asking, *"When and where is this problem not present?"*

Or if you find that someone is overly concerned about a situation that they have no responsibility for, and little control over, be sure to remind them, *"That isn't your pig to wrestle."*

However you choose to use it, having read the fable, we trust that you are now much more able to consistently find your way back out of the pig pen. Our sincere hope is that by having the skills to clean your own and other people's thinking, you can create the change that you and the wider world truly needs.

If having read the book you have found a more empowering way to view a problematic situation, we'd really love to hear from you. Please do get in touch and send us your story- you can find our email address, website and twitter at the end of the book.

PROBLEM CLEANING OVERVIEW

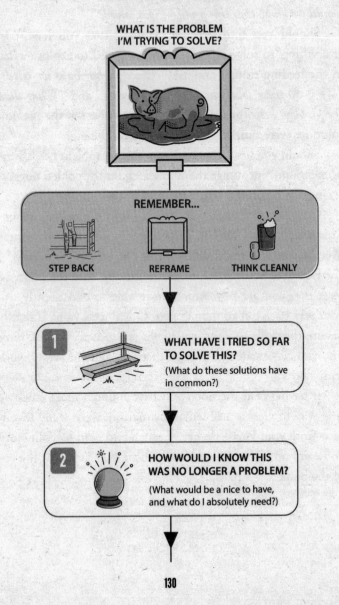

**WHAT IS THE PROBLEM
I'M TRYING TO SOLVE?**

REMEMBER...

STEP BACK   REFRAME   THINK CLEANLY

1   **WHAT HAVE I TRIED SO FAR
TO SOLVE THIS?**
(What do these solutions have
in common?)

2   **HOW WOULD I KNOW THIS
WAS NO LONGER A PROBLEM?**
(What would be a nice to have,
and what do I absolutely need?)

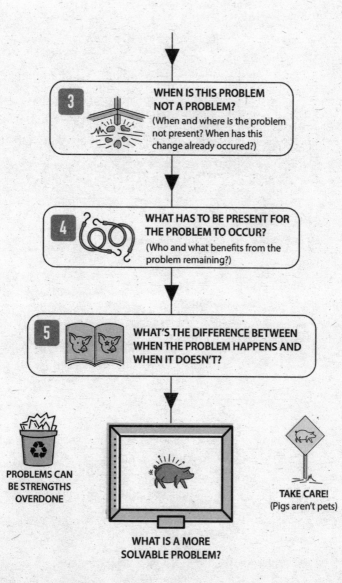

3 WHEN IS THIS PROBLEM NOT A PROBLEM?
(When and where is the problem not present? When has this change already occured?)

4 WHAT HAS TO BE PRESENT FOR THE PROBLEM TO OCCUR?
(Who and what benefits from the problem remaining?)

5 WHAT'S THE DIFFERENCE BETWEEN WHEN THE PROBLEM HAPPENS AND WHEN IT DOESN'T?

PROBLEMS CAN BE STRENGTHS OVERDONE

WHAT IS A MORE SOLVABLE PROBLEM?

TAKE CARE!
(Pigs aren't pets)

ACKNOWLEDGEMENTS

There were many times during the writing of this book when it felt like we were wrestling with a filthy pig.

Writing it has been a process of problem solving in itself. Over the course of numerous drafts and total rewrites, we've experimented with different ways of conveying the spirit of problem cleaning in a format that is both accessible and enjoyable. We hope we've gone some way towards achieving this end, but we leave it to you, the reader, to be the judge of that.

For their support in getting us to here, we'd like to extend special thanks to a number of key individuals.

Firstly, to our families and friends. Without your support we wouldn't even be considering writing something of this nature, never mind actually being able to achieve it.

Thank you to Georgie, Matilda, and Eliza—you three are truly the centre of my [PL's] world. I know there have been plenty of times when I've brought pigs home and left trotter prints through our hallway. Thanks for your ongoing belief and support throughout this project. I promise that we'll try to not take quite so long on the next one!

Thanks to Sarah, Harry, and Max for being a constant inspiration to me [MB], and for keeping me out of the pig pen. I hope that at some point in your lives, the thinking and ideas in this book will help you when you find yourself stuck. If that happens then all of this will have been worthwhile. Finally, thanks to Pink Floyd for their genius and introducing me to the perils of 'flying pigs'.

We'd also like to thank the numerous people who have shaped our thinking over the years, either in person or through their writing. The list is far too long to include everyone, but special thanks must go to the following people, whose contributions were most valuable in crafting this framework:

Gregory Bateson for his mind, his writings, and his thinking around the cybernetic explanation of behaviour.

Milton Erickson for his pioneering work in brief approaches to therapy.

Bill O'Hanlon for his ability to convey his thinking around possibilities in accessible language.

Dr. James Wilk for his expertise and writings around change and shifting contexts.

Ludwig Wittgenstein for his seminal work on philosophy, language games, and how we bewitch ourselves.

Steve de Shazer for his pioneering approach to solution focussed approaches.

Spencer Johnson for his demonstration of how to use a simple fable and metaphor to convey practically applicable principles to the reader.

We owe an immense amount to our editor, Sara Starbuck. Without your talent, your passion, and your patience, we'd never have crafted this story. Your creativity and humour throughout the process of developing this fable have been greatly appreciated and valued.

A huge debt is also owed to a valued colleague and dear friend of ours, Dr Tim Pitt. Tim, your 'passionate curiosity' and 'confident humility' has got us both out of the pig pen numerous times as we tried to wrestle with the principles underpinning this book.

Finally, we'd like to thank a gentleman by the name of Dave Hewitt. Thank you for introducing us to characters such as Arthur and Eric. Their charm and the problems they faced in the farmyard helped us greatly in getting us to this point. Without your support at a critical juncture, this book may never have arrived in its present form.

ABOUT THE AUTHORS

Pete Lindsay, PhD

Pete is a performance psychologist and cofounder of Mindflick. He has spent his career striving to make psychology accessible, tangible, and relevant to high performers. His work has been featured in the *Times*, the *Guardian*, and leading research journals.

Previously the head of psychology at the English Institute of Sport, Pete worked with many of Great Britain's Olympic teams. Alongside his work in the corporate domain with CEOs and Michelin-starred chefs, he works with a leading Premier League football club.

Mark Bawden, PhD

Before cofounding Mindflick, Mark spent twenty years as a performance psychologist, which saw him work across elite sport, education, health, and business.

Mark has applied his "strength-based approach" to performance enhancement throughout professional and Olympic sport, contributing to five Olympic Games, including being Team GB Head Psychologist at the London 2012 Games.

Mark worked with the England cricket team for seven years and was subsequently head of psychology at the ECB.

In order to succeed, every organisation needs to get the very best out of its people and teams.

We've now applied Pig Wrestling (also known as 'Short-Cycle Coaching') across a range of organisations, teaching the principles of problem cleaning to individuals and groups. Alongside our work within these organisations, we also offer 2-day accreditation courses for individuals who would like to bring this approach into their professional roles.

The problems that we wrestle with, and the solutions we typically try, are inherently linked to how we see our world. Understanding our own, and other people's 'Behavioural Style' and 'Mindset' is a powerful way to avoid wrestling with ill-defined problems in the first place. This is why we developed 'Spotlight', a personality profiling tool designed with performance in mind, which is now being used by a wide range of high performing organisations across the globe.

We run 3-day Spotlight accreditation workshops, investing heavily in making sure that Accredited Spotlight Practitioners have everything they need to make Spotlight and problem cleaning a success in their context.

Learn more: mindflick.co.uk
Contact us: switch@mindflick.co.uk
Follow us: @mindflick

Mindflick Ltd
3, The Barn
Hathersage Hall Business Centre
Main Road
Hathersage
S32 1BB